WRITTEN BY LATRE'

The Truth Women hate To Hear

MIDNITE DAKOTA
PUBLISHING

This book is dedicated to Jackie Medley. We had so many talks. I wish I could remember every word. I know you're with Pops, and your suffering is over. I focus on that, though I wish you were here. Without you, I don't exist. You are the inspiration behind my dreams and the motivation behind my actions. My tears are never wasted when they fall over you.

Rest Easy, My Love. You will always be the prettiest girl in the world! - Tre'

Contents

Foreword	iii
Acknowledgments	iv
Introduction	1
Accountawhat?	5
But Is He Searching For You?	20
Don't Be Delusional	27
Drive Is Attractive, A "Bad Bitch" Is Not	39
Dressed for Attention, Crying for Respect	44
A Girls Girl	50
The Power of Vulnerability	57
Emotional Baggage Is Annoying	64
The Unsettling Truth	70
Having A Baby Decreases Your Value	77
High Body Counts Are Disgusting	82
Don't Fight Back, Just Leave!	87
Lady In The Streets, But A...	93
Can You Be Trusted?	99
Using A Man Is Dangerous	106
Having a "Lil Attitude" Is Not Sexy	111
Yes! Flirting And Dancing Is Cheating!	119
Conclusion	125
Glossary	130
Bibliography	135
Recommended Reading	137

Foreword

This isn't just another book you skim through and forget about. This is something real. Every page was written with intention because I wanted to give you more than advice, I wanted to give you game. The kind of knowledge people usually keep to themselves.

I've lived what I'm talking about. This isn't theory. It's experience. It's lessons I had to learn the hard way, and now I'm passing them on so you don't have to go through the same struggles. Whether you take one thing from this or the whole blueprint, my goal is simple: to help you level up.

So, as you dive into these chapters, keep an open mind. Some of what I say might challenge you. Some of it might even make you uncomfortable. That's good. Growth never feels comfortable at first. But if you apply what's inside these pages, I promise you'll see results.

Let's get to it.

Acknowledgments

First and foremost, all glory goes to Jehovah. There has never been a time I approached Him in prayer and didn't receive what I asked for. My prayers are like superpowers, every blessing in my life is proof of His grace.

To my Momma: Woman, I love you so much, I don't know what in the world to do. I'm nothing without you, and I owe you everything! Thank you.

To my exes: you inspired this book in ways you'll never understand. Especially Dionna's bitch ass. Sometimes pain teaches you more than love ever could, and for that, I'm grateful.

To my family: Fuck You!

To everyone who gave me game, motivation, or just kept it real when I needed it, thank you.

Lastly, to every reader holding this book, you matter. Whether you bought it, borrowed it, or just stumbled on it, thank you for giving me your time. My hope is that these pages give you something real you can use.

Introduction

Fair warning: This book, though filled with real-life insight and knowledge, will trigger many folks. Hello! My name is LaTre', and I come in peace! My goal is to help, not hurt, but if you get hurt, that may help! Okay, let's get into it! What do women seem to hate the most out of all the things they seem to hate? Well to some the answer may be easy, and three points to you if you got it right! The Answer: The truth. They hate facing the truth about anything, not all women but most. Facing the truth also falls into the same category as taking accountability. They just can't do it. If you have a woman in your life who can, then that's the woman you marry! If not marry then she is at least worth you putting the effort in trying to make the relationship work. A woman like that is a dime a dozen.

This book is not created to bash women, but I will let you know some of the truths I tell and the blunt way in which I choose to tell them may hurt some feelings. Some women will read this book and say things like "Who Hurt You?" or "Misogynistic". They may even go as far as saying stupid shit like " Little Dick Energy." Whatever, that's just them taking the information being provided and instead of processing it in a logical and informative manner with an understanding of how it may help them, choosing to be emotional and offended… towards the truth I might add. Then, they project those negative feelings towards the person providing the information. A wise man once said, "I do not get offended by facts." An even wiser woman said, "Only fools think with their emotions."

I focus on these words of wisdom while writing this book, knowing not everyone will be as accepting of the information this book has to offer. Let me be clear before we start. When this book drops, I'm gonna be getting called every name. I know the disrespect is coming. I won't be surprised by it. I'm ready for it.

There's a line people credit to Socrates:
    "When the debate is lost, slander becomes the tool of the loser." This means that when someone realizes they can't win an argument with logic or facts, they resort to insults, personal attacks, or manipulation instead. Instead of proving their point, they try to discredit you. Another quote by Socrates that could be applied:

"The secret of change is to focus all of your energy not on fighting the old, but on building the new." That's my stance. I'm not here to fight labels. I'm here to build new standards, new habits, new results. No debates. No drama. Results. If you want comfort, close the book.

If you want change, keep reading.

Accountability, intention, presentation, receipts. That's what you're getting here.

So, with that being said, let's get into it, shall we? Last warning, ladies: keep your emotions at the door or, in this instance, the cover! If you can handle blunt truth and want results, not excuses, this book will give you the game and the mirror. Open your mind and dive in!

Accountawhat?

Accountability! Keeping the title of this chapter short and simple. That will change the further along in the book we get.

Let's be honest, you know what this is about. Making a scene, then being wrong, but not apologizing. Doing the most, hurting your man's feelings, yes men have feelings, disrespecting your man, and not being woman enough to make it right. Attempting to slide past it or thinking that not addressing it solve the problem no goodness well you required an apology if the shoe was near the other foot.

Traffic Finding out you're wrong about something and attempting to move past it without addressing the negativity you brought to the situation is not only immature but also a good way to show you don't value your relationship. Accusing your man of cheating and being wrong, then turning it on him in some way.

To sum it all up just creating a situation out of nothing and then finding out that your truth is not THE truth, but not accepting it or admitting it. What is that? Please tell me! Is it ego or maybe even pride? Let me know because it's something I've never been able to figure out. Taking accountability is the beginning of solving a problem. Women will claim to be problem solvers but can't solve the problem of their own failing relationships. It could be a lot simpler than they make it though. Admitting when you're wrong could save your relationship. Even make your relationship stronger. It will be a major contributor to getting the love of your life back or developing a healthier love within the relationship that you're currently working to maintain.

Regrets

I've talked to too many women who regret how they handled things in their past relationships. When they tell me their stories, it always has something to do with them taking an issue too far or creating an issue out of thin air, then doing the most, even once they realize they're the ones wrong in the situation. For whatever reason, they would rather say something like, "Well, if you didn't do this, then I wouldn't have done this," or "You know I don't like it when." Even going as far as saying

7

stupid shit like, "Even when I'm wrong, I'm right." Is it really that difficult to admit when you're wrong? That's a question I ask them. Their response is a simple and depressing, YES! Women would rather be right then be happy

I'll say that one more time… women would rather be right then be happy. All too often I see women are willing to sacrifice their entire relationship even families over them attempting to make a point that isn't even accurate. Here is an example: A man and a woman go on vacation. They have an excursion planned, a beautiful boat ride! He tells his woman that it will be cold and windy on the water. He suggests that she wears a sweater. She ignores his suggestion. He wears a sweater for himself. They are now on the boat. And she is sitting there angle with her arms crossed and a nasty attitude. Why does she have an attitude you might ask? Because the main man refused to give her his sweater. You tell me is the man right or wrong? Well, depending on your level of education, you might acknowledge this as him attempting to lead her, and she did not want to be led. Now inspired of acknowledging that she was wrong. She's willing to ruin the entire vacation. A trip that could've been a beautiful core memory and experience for both of them. It has just fit itself in the category of "we don't get along" or "we always argue". Guess who the woman is gonna blame for these problems. Exactly! There will be zero accountability and zero reflection in the part she played in that situation.

Just think about it for a second. A human being walking around thinking they are never wrong even when it's proven that they are. That is a dangerous personality trait and a hell of a princess complex. A few questions to consider would greatly improve your way of thinking when dealing with these situations. Questions like: What matters the most to you, being right all the time or your relationship with your person? Do you care if your words or actions hurt your partner? Do you claim to be a mature woman? Well, let's be honest, real maturity within a woman who is ready for a mature man has everything to do with her ability to support her man and do her part in building the home and making their relationship work. This includes swallowing your pride, especially when you're in the wrong, and you're aware that you're in the wrong. Don't be so prideful that you would be willing to give up a good man or healthy relationship just because you're embarrassed to be wrong. If you have the right man by your side, he won't make you feel any way about it. If anything, he will applaud you and be thankful for your humbleness and desire for peace and security.

Pride Is In The Way

Here is another truth: A man will give up his happiness for his relationship, but a woman will give up her relationship for her happiness. Swallowing your pride prevents so much! Like going to bed angry! Think about it ladies, have you ever gone to bed angry with your man and with him upset at you, then as you're laying there realizing you were wrong and the fight was minor and could have been prevented and yet still do nothing, you lay there in silence. All you want at that moment is for your man to turn over and hold you, cuddle you as if the situation never happened, but unfortunately, you did too much to prove a point you knew you were wrong about. That cuddle never comes and now it's the next day and he's still upset and now you're upset at the fact that he is still upset because you convinced yourself that he would be over it in the morning without you having to do anything. Yea, I know you have, most women do. Let me ask you something, how do you expect him to feel better or get over a situation if you don't do your part to make the situation better?

Here is the thing about problems ladies, you can ignore them, walk away from them, take all the time you need to fake think and process shit, but when you come back, they'll still be there, they're just gonna be big as hell. Unfortunately, it's gonna get to a certain point where you don't even deserve an easy-to-get-past situation, you ruined that for yourself. You know your ass probably crossed a line. Truth is the argument could have been over once you first realized you were doing the most. Another truth is that most women realize mid-argument that they're wrong and doing too much, but will deadass think to themselves "Well I've already done all this so I can't back down now."

My promise to you is that if you continue this behavior your relationship will end and it will be your fault, and if you do not fix this behavior every relationship you enter will end the same and you will continue to have this princess complex while simultaneously pushing the blame onto your partners. You've got to teach yourself to bring something different to the table. You've got to find and be that something else that will help your relationship grow. Something different than what the typical everyday woman is offering. Something that your dream man can't just find anywhere but can only have with you. What is your something else?

Locked in. I studied your voice and wrote this in pure BluntTrè. Short punches. No fluff. A little profanity where it earns the hit. Drop this right after your question, "What is your something else?" Split in two parts so it flows clean.

No more lying to yourself.
"Something else" ain't lashes, filters, or a new caption.
It ain't the bag on your arm or the body you rented for summer.
"Something else" is what's left when the lights cut off, when sex is off the table, when life swings on you and there's no audience.

It's the proof.
Not the promise.
The pattern.
Not the post.

Read slow and check yourself.

Character.

Do you do right when nobody's clapping.
If you talk loud in public and whisper "my bad" in private, your character is on clearance.

Consistency.

Can he trust Tuesday to look like Monday.
   If your mood is a roulette wheel, nobody is betting their future on you.

Competence.

Do you run your life like an adult.
   Bills. Body. Bedroom. Bank. Calendar.
   If you can't manage you, why should he hand you any piece of him.

Care.

Not mothering. Not nagging. Care.
   You notice needs before they turn into problems.
   You speak life without acting like his boss.

Communication.

Say what you feel without swinging.
   Short. Clear. Specific.
   No weaponized tears. No silent treatment. No three-day punishments.

Control.

Self control is sexy.

Your tongue. Your spending. Your phone. Your appetite.

If everything you do is impulse, your future is chaos. Grown men clock that. Then they dodge it.

Now let me hurt your feelings for a second.

If "pretty" is your whole personality, that's surface.

If "badder than the next girl" is your identity, that's a score-board with no game.

If "independent" is your wall, where's the door. Independence is great, but partnership still needs an entrance.

"Something else" is the door.

It's how a man enters your world and finds order, warmth, peace, fun, growth and respect sitting at the same table.

It's how you move when nobody's watching.

How you apologize without theater.

How you disagree without burning the house down.

Look at your patterns.

- If your phone is full of mess, your life is probably full of mess. Clean it.
- If your friends run on drama, your relationship will inherit it. Tighten the circle.
- If your body is last on your list, your energy will be last in the relationship. Fix your health.
- If your money is short because your discipline is short, you'll feel small next to a disciplined man. Learn a budget.

- If you only pray, read, or journal when you're hurt, you're reactive, not growing. Set a daily time. No excuses.

"Something else" is not a product. It's a pattern you repeat.
    Quiet. Solid. Boring in the best way.
    Repeat it long enough and the room calls you valuable without you asking.

Receipt: Pretty pulls attention. Patterns keep a man.

Mirror Check: Without sex, makeup, or social media, would he still chase you for your patterns

You don't need a new personality.
    You need a plan.
    Simple. Grown. No excuses.

1) Build your baseline.
    Four pillars. Health, money, home, mindset.
    Set one non-negotiable for each.

- Health, move 45 minutes, five days a week.
- Money, write every purchase, weekly review, no ghost swipes.
- Home, 15-minute reset nightly, sink empty, clothes put away.
- Mindset, 20 minutes reading or prayer daily, phone off.

Do it 30 days straight.
    No speeches. Just work.
    Your energy changes. Your mouth calms down. Your patience

grows.

Men notice that more than eyeliner.

2) Create a respect routine.
Respect is not a feeling. It's a schedule.

- Morning check-in if you're together. Two sentences, your plan for the day.
- If you're wrong, say it by noon. Never sleep on your mess.
- Weekly, one phone-free date or hour. If money's tight, walk and talk. Effort is the currency.

Respect routines kill guesswork.
Guesswork breeds insecurity.
Insecurity breeds chaos.
Chaos kills attraction.

3) Set boundary sentences.
No screams. No essays. Three lines.

- "I'm not okay with that. Here's what I need instead."
- "I want to keep this calm. Let's take ten and come back."
- "I hear you. Here's what I'm doing on my end."

Short. Clear. Calm.
Boundaries let you respect you without disrespecting him.

4) Practice conflict clean-up.
Conflict ain't the problem. Filthy clean-up is.
Use this:

- Name it, "I raised my voice."
- Own it, "That was on me."
- Repair it, "Here's how I'll handle it next time."
- Replace it, actually do the new behavior next time.

That last step is where love lives or dies.
   He'll believe your pattern, not your speech.

5) Protect your peace like rent money.
   Loud life, tired love.

- One hour a day off social media. No other people's chaos.
- One room stays clean, always. Peace needs a place to sit.
- One person gets benched if they bring mess. Even family.
- One weekly sabbath. Rest is discipline, not laziness.

6) Make femininity a practice, not an outfit.
   Soft is not silent. Submissive is not small.
   Femininity is control without combat.

- Listen to understand, not to load a comeback.
- Receive help without acting insulted.
- Celebrate his wins without shrinking yourself.

When you live like this, men breathe easier around you.
   Breathing room builds desire.

7) Build real-world social proof.
   Online likes are cheap. Real respect is earned.

- Be the friend who shows up, not the friend who posts.

- Be the auntie who keeps her word, not the auntie with excuses.
- Be the coworker who's early, not the one always "on the way."

Reputation is "something else" people can verify without you selling it.

8) Add delight.
   You're not a drill sergeant. Be fun sometimes.

- Learn his two little favorites and hit them weekly. A snack. A song. A note.
- Learn one new skill each quarter. Salsa. Steak. Stretching. Spreadsheets.
- Plan a surprise in his love language, not yours.

Delight is generosity without keeping score.
   Sweet goes a long way when your standards are strong.

9) Keep your body a priority.
   This ain't perfection. It's respect.

- Move. Sweat. Hydrate. Sleep.
- Eat more real food than fake food.
- Wear clothes that fit the body you have while you build the body you want.

Do it for you first.
   Confidence is quiet power.
   Quiet power is attractive.

10) Close the gap between your talk and your calendar.

If your mouth says "wife," your schedule should whisper the same.

- Discipline when nobody reminds you.
- Promises kept when it's inconvenient.
- Effort you can see, not just feel.

That's the line between grown girls and grown women.
  Grown girls talk.
  Grown women implement.

Common traps that kill "something else"

- Perfection thinking. You miss a day, you quit. Stop it. Reset by the next hour.
- Audience thinking. You only try when eyes are on you. Kill that. Live it when nobody's looking.
- Rescue thinking. You think a man will fix what you refuse to face. He won't. If he tries, you'll resent him.

What a man actually sees when it's real

- Calm in conflict, not chaos.
- Soft hands, strong standards.
- A home that feels like a charger, not a war zone.
- A woman who says "my fault" and does not rerun the same episode.
- A pattern that holds, month after month.

That's wife energy. That's forever energy.

Not loud, not thirsty, not perfect. Consistent.

Receipt: Your "something else" is not what you post. It's what you repeat.

Do A Drill

- Today: Pick your four pillars. One non-negotiable each. Tell nobody. Do them.
- This week: One phone-free hour with him, one hour off social for you.
- This month: Track every conflict. Count how many you cleaned the same day. Aim for all.

Bottom line:
  "Something else" is proof.
  Not a vibe, not a caption, not a costume.
  Live it long enough and you won't have to demand respect. You'll command it.
  And if a man can't handle that level of clarity, good.
  Your door only opens for grown men. You just gotta be the woman a grown man is looking for.

But Is He Searching For You?

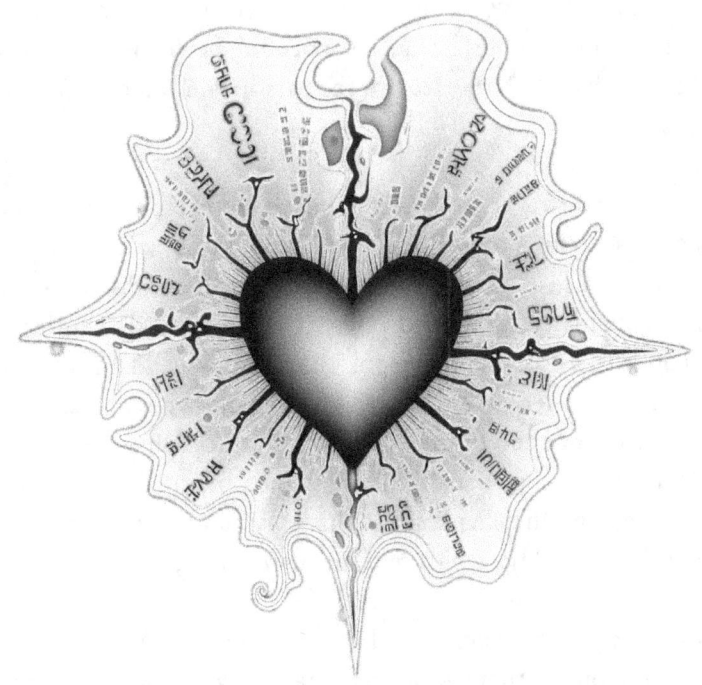

No, seriously! Answer the question! I'm sure most of you would say yes. There goes that delusion again. I swear you all be tripping. Truth is, no one is the person our dream person is looking for, man or woman. Even our dream person has a dream person, and that person will always be the person of our dreams. No matter how close a person comes to fitting the description of our dream person something will always be missing. They'll either lack one thing or have too much of something else.

This does not mean we cannot attract or find our dream person by becoming the type of person our dream person wants to be with. There will always be negatives in life, and there's no such thing as perfection, so expecting perfection is insane. Working hard to be perfect for the person you want is perfectly reasonable.

Here are a few ways to become the type of person your dream man is searching for. Number 1 is to read this book and apply what you read and learn in your day-to-day life. This may seem like a shameless plug, and yes part of it is, but the truth is I wrote this book with a purpose in mind. The goal is to help women who feel like they can't be helped, who are ready to make a change and to stop blaming others for why they cannot get and/or keep a man. To teach women the truth about their ways and give them a mirror so that they may truly reflect upon themselves and their past or even current actions and lifestyle.

Most women hate being told the truth about themselves, but if you're one of them and can manage to get past the feelings then you can learn something that may lead you to the life you THINK you deserve. I want to get you to the point of you actually deserving that life. No second guesses, and no being looked at like you're crazy from the outside world. No more believing you deserve anything; belief is a doubt! You'll know, nothing more nothing less. No more delusion!

Where Is He?

Once you've applied what you've learned from this book and feel as though you're ready to test it out, move on to the next step. Step number 2 would be to go where the man you want is.

Is the man of your dreams on the street corner slanging dope? Maybe he is living in his momma's basement selling weed. Does he go to the club every other night? Are you searching for quality or are you just searching? Are you trying to be found by your Dream man or just be found by a man? Well if he is in any of those places I mentioned above you won't have to look hard for him.

I want you to think outside the box though. Is the man of your dreams in good shape? Then try getting a gym membership and searching there. Let's go a little deeper though. You want a Planet Fitness type of Man or a LA Fitness type of man. You can tell a lot about a man and his pockets and lifestyle based on the gym he goes to. Both gyms come at two very different price points. Both have two very different qualities of men working out there. Do you want a man who shops at Save-A-Lot or a man who shops at Whole Foods? Well, the truth is if you're a Save-A-Lot shopping woman, you'll find yourself a Save-A-Lot shopping man. You can't afford to shop at Whole Foods? Then maybe you should work on building your own self up first so you can shop at a quality grocery store before expecting a Whole Foods Man to wife a Save-A-Lot woman.

Is the man of your dreams educated? Try going back to school and searching the college campus. Many men go back to college even after they've graduated. They aim to increase their knowledge and revenue and search for a woman with similar goals and values. Why can't that woman be you? You may even try searching the local library.

Does your dream man have money? Does he have a Bank Of

America or Navy Federal Credit Union account? There's a difference, not necessarily in the amount of money they have but in the quality of the man that uses these banks. The next time you need to go to the bank try going inside instead of the drive-thru. The same goes for the places you eat at. Even if you go to a fast food restaurant, there's nothing wrong with that. Just try walking inside versus the drive-thru. When you isolate yourself in your care you shield yourself from opportunities.

That man who walked up to you a few months ago and tried to get your number turns out he had a business plan and is about to become a successful entrepreneur and would have treated you like a queen. He may have even been your dream guy. Why'd you reject him? You didn't like how he was dressed? He had messy hair? Did he talk a certain way? Was his teeth jacked up? Were you scared? You hate talking to dudes on the subway or whatever your reasoning was, you blocked your own blessings. May your search continue.

Regardless, the point I'm trying to make is to go where the man you're searching for is because the woman he wants is already there. Ask yourself a few simple questions. In fact, let's turn it into an exercise.

The Exercise

I want you to write down what your dream guy does in his day-to-day life. What would you want his schedule to look like? Then I want you to do the same things you would want your dream guy to be doing. That's how you're going to attract him. That's how you're going to become the woman he is searching for.

Does he wake up at 5 AM and go for a run at the park? Then get your ass up, go run at the park at 5 AM and you might just find the man that's gonna take care of you for the rest of your life! Does he shop at Hot Topic or Express? Costco or BJ's? McDonalds or Five Guys? Is he religious? Does he go to a place of worship every Sunday? Where does he go? Is it a Baptist Church or a Kingdom Hall of Jehovah's Witnesses? Is he in the suburbs or the city? Where are you? Take the train and ask yourself if he's the guy with the suit on with the briefcase or the guy with the cigarette behind his ear sagging his pants.

My point is, if you're not where your dream man is if you're not advertising yourself as someone your dream man is searching for, then how do you expect your dream man to find you? Next time you're hungry, go sit at Panera Bread. Next time you need groceries go to the Whole Foods in that nice neighborhood. Simple changes like that make all the difference in the quality of man you attract in your life. Go have lunch between 12 and 2 at a nice restaurant in a business district. Why? If you're searching for a man with a good job, stability, and a decent income, he probably works in the business district and goes on break around that time! That will be the restaurant he walks into to have his lunch. You can find yourself a lawyer like that! Go eat at a hospital cafeteria. It's open to the public and the food is good quality. You might find a doctor! Go where these men are at. That doctor is not gonna be at the clubs. You should even be more selective about where you go and have drinks. Does he like sports? After work hours, head to Buffalo Wild Wings, where you know a game is playing, and sit at the bar.

He might come and sit right next to you, all you gotta do is be there. I'm sure you got the picture by now.

Be His Dream Woman

Remember despite being in the places this so-called dream man of yours is at, you must also be the woman he would want to be with. That's very important and you can't forget it. For that change to come you may need to take time away from the dating scene and be by yourself for a bit. Just to teach and train yourself. Men want women that allow themselves to be women. Women who play the role, not try to be the man in the relationship. If a man has to try too hard to be masculine because your masculinity is too overbearing he'll move on. Men love femininity!

Learn yourself and how to manage your own life and habits before rushing to deal with someone else's. Are you the type of person who changes the toilet paper roll when you see that it's empty or leaves it for the next person to change? Simple things like that speak a lot about who you are as a person. Are you a lover or a fighter? Do you fight for what you love? Do you give up when shit gets a little rough? There has to be something else that's beautifully different about you that makes you stand out to your dream man. All you gotta do is find it and amplify it! What is your something else?

Don't Be Delusional

One of a man's least favorite types of women worldwide is the delusional one. These are the women who think the world revolves around them. They feel as though the sun and moon rise and set simply because they exist on the earth. This type of woman is probably the most dangerous, and we will discuss her in this book.

Her princess complex makes her blind to reality. She thinks every man alive or dead wants her for no other reason but for the fact that she has a vagina. She thinks she can get any man in the world, and if a man doesn't want her he must be gay. She believes in stupid shit like a man needs to pay for every piece of food that enters her mouth. She has a hard time showing gratitude for even the simplest of things. She also believes that pussy is a good enough payment for every act of service she receives. That is a top-tier delusion if you've ever seen it. If you're one of these women, I hope your purpose for reading this book is to recognize it and be ready to make a change.

Story Time

I had a girlfriend some years back who had a mild case of this complex. She was pretty self-righteous and had a "Boss Bitch" mindset. We will dive deeper into that "Boss Bitch" subject a little later! Anyways, she was never the type to say thank you for anything, rather she would complain and find something negative in even the most thoughtful acts. Once, I bought her some snow tires for her car, salt, sand, a window scraper, and a snow shovel. I just wanted her to be prepared for wintertime, and she wasn't going to make these purchases herself. Plus I hated worrying about her knowing that a snowfall was coming. So I made these purchases for her just in case I wasn't with her. I wanted her to be properly prepared for winter situations. It would give me some peace knowing that she was okay and not sliding all over the roads with the bald tires she previously had.

Instead of saying "Thank You" or being grateful, which by the way was not a requirement, I didn't do it for a "Thank You" I did it because it was my job as a man to make sure my woman was okay and taken care of, she instead decided to say to me "In my last relationship I didn't even have to drive, I was a passenger princess". I don't think I need to tell you that the relationship between us eventually came to an end. I was able to move past that situation, but eventually, her strong sense of delusion became unbearable. I've also been the type of man to stay even when things got hard because I was raised to believe that when things get rough, you don't run, you work it out. Unlike her, who was raised to be a track star, if you know what I mean?

A few years before her, I was involved in another relationship, and this woman tried to convince me that Valentine's Day was a day for the man to celebrate his woman, show how much he loved her, and give her gifts. Silly me, I thought Valentine's Day was a day for couples to express their love for one another and spread love across their community and family. I be tripp'n sometimes, I guess. That relationship didn't last either.

Can you figure out what these two women had in common? Besides my poor choice in picking partners... A princess complex! Delusion at work within both of these women. I made the mistake of telling one of these women about her delusion, and oh my, was that a mistake I didn't hear the end of until the relationship finally died. I was confused. I didn't lie, I didn't insult her, I didn't yell or curse or degrade her. Yet she displayed anger towards me that never went away, no matter the good times or the bad. She still passively brings it up a year later, no matter the situation or conversation. It wasn't until later, once the relationship had been over for a while that I had time to sit a ponder on some of my past life experiences that then realized what truly happened. I told her a truth she didn't want to hear. Something she not only did not expect from me, but she wasn't prepared to hear let alone accept. It was the truth nonetheless, the truth women hate to hear.

What Is Delusion?

My definition of delusion would be to convince yourself to believe that something is reality when all the evidence and proof exist around you that it's not. The Merriam-Webster Dictionary's definition of delusion is "A persistent false psychotic belief regarding the self or persons or objects outside the self that is maintained despite indisputable evidence to the contrary."

A lot of women fear the truth, not just being told the truth by someone else, but also telling the truth to themselves. This would require them to accept the truth, accepting reality, something most women are not ready for. They get comfortable in the fairy tale world they've created for themselves. For them, leaving that Neverland would be as close to death as they could get without actually dying. It takes a strong woman to clothe herself with a new personality.

Too many women wish to be seen as perfect or the best option any man could want. Being shown that they're not and accepting that goes against everything they've been brought up to believe about themselves.

It's Da Daddy's Fault

Not every single time is it the father's fault, but there is a strong truth behind that statement. You have a large group of fathers who love their daughters so much that they raise them to believe no man is good enough for them. They raise them to believe that they are the most perfect beings in all of existence. Is this

31

wrong? Absolutely! Most do this because they are aware of how they have abused and mistreated women. How they've done women dirty hopping from girl to girl and turning nice girls into sluts like it's nothing, then moving on with their life without a care in the world. Then they have a baby girl and catch that eye-opening experience that one day this beautiful baby that fits oh so perfectly in their arms will be old enough to have sex. The thought of that and what she could turn into if she allows the wrong man or men to enter inside of her scares the soul out of him as a father. So now they begin the princess treatment or princess school. Creating a standard so high that no man could ever reach. Got their daughter thinking that no man could ever compare to her daddy, but in reality, your daddy is teaching you to reject men who he was once like. Now she's "Daddy's Little Girl."

Truly sad. Look, I'm not saying there's anything wrong with creating standards in your daughter or even treating her like a princess, but raising them to believe that no man will ever be good enough for them and they are the most perfect piece of human flesh that ever existed in the oh so imperfect world will do nothing but create a future problem for the young girl that the father can not yet see. Not until she's crying to him at the age of 35 because, for whatever strange reason, she can't seem to keep a man, and he wants some grandkids.

Ladies, I encourage you all to have standards! Please don't just settle for any ole thing out here! At the same time, don't walk this earth thinking your shit doesn't stink. That is the highly discouraged part. Thinking your fantasy or dream guy will appear and scoop you off of your feet when you're not even worthy of that type of treatment is crazy. What makes you think your dream guy would want you anyway?

Are You Worthy?

Do you pay your bills on time? Are you good with money management? Do you expect him to take care of all the finances? Are you still on your parents' insurance? Are your hair and nails kept up? Are you all-natural? Do you wear a lot of makeup? Do you already have kids? Have you had a lot of sexual partners? Are you currently on birth control? Why? You be letting nigga's nut inside of you just cause you on birth control? Do you have a job? Can you keep a job? Is your main source of income from the government? Do you smoke cigarettes? Do you have a history of drug abuse? Do you have a lot of male friends? Do you have a straight male best friend? Do you work out? Do you have a healthy diet? Can you bear children? Will the children come out healthy? What's your mental health history like? Do you have any real standards for yourself in your day-to-day life? How is your hygiene? Do you brush your teeth in the morning? How often do you get yeast infections? Does your vagina have a smell? Have you convinced yourself that that smell is normal? Are you perfect for no other reason besides the facts that you say you are? Don't be delusional!

You expect a real man but you're not even a real woman! And since we're here... let's talk about that equal pay thing. There was this video that went viral, a woman on a construction site struggling to swing a damn sledgehammer. She could barely get it over her head, let alone use it properly. And the comments were full of women screaming "Equal pay!" in the same breath. How you demanding equal pay for unequal performance? That's delusion.

See, y'all want the paycheck that comes with hard-ass labor, but not the calluses, the sweat, the 10-hour shifts in 90-degree heat, or the risk of falling off a scaffold. Meanwhile, women have the option to sell their bodies online and become rich damn near overnight, something most men could never do successfully. You can literally do nothing with your life, and a man will still come along and change it for you. That's a luxury men don't get.

Women get rich off existing. Off being cute. Off having a fat ass or doing a lil' spin on TikTok. Some of y'all be the laziest humans alive, but think y'all deserve CEO-level respect just for waking up. Then you got the nerve to talk about "equality." Equal pay ain't the problem, it's the lack of equal effort that nobody wants to talk about.

You just want some rich baller type of man to come and save you. Spend his last on you and somehow never run out of money while treating you like you never do anything wrong. I promise you that's not reality, that's a delusion! You gotta know better to be a better momma! I'm not trying to degrade you, I'm trying to open your mind to what's real!

The reality is Micheal B. Jordan is not about to pull up to the Taco Bell drive-through you're working at, stare into your eyes, and tell you to put the headset and hot sauce down and get in the limo. Unfortunately, when you're delusional that's exactly how you think, that's also exactly how you end up 40 years old and single, telling folks you don't want a man, but we both know that ain't the truth. Might even end up with a few kids along the way. Still believe you got a shot with Chris Brown Or Drake. Delusion at its best.

Humble Yourself

Only three perfect people walked this earth, and you were not and are not one of them. Help yourself, humble yourself. A good way to learn is by reading the Bible. I know some of you are gonna hate that, but whether you believe in the Bible's teaching or not it is a fact that the Bible sets a standard for how a woman should present herself. God gives you the guide and information you need to make the changes you need to make to attract the man you want to attract. It gives you the expectations Jehovah has for you and is a good starting point for change.

I know it's challenging. It's not like you have the best role models. You got Meghan Thee Stallion, Cardi B, Beyonce', Saweetie, Doechii, Glorilla and Ice Spice, just to name a few. These women do not have your best interests at heart. Their job is to sell records, and they have figured out the best way to do this by capitalizing on the audience's emotions. Which is made up of mostly women. They make male hate songs, break-up songs, songs that promote a woman to be and stay single, songs that tell you you don't need a man, while at the same time slowly convincing you that you don't want one either. Now you wanna be a city girl outside in Miami. Here is another truth: When y'all be saying "Miami not ready for us!" Thats delusion... yall act like Miami never seen a few hoes before…Anyway, these women are happy in love enjoying their relationship and the money they made from your streams. Now the new world we live in is being formed by their music and a new type of female, a more dangerous one.

Female independence has taken over. Not saying there's anything wrong with that, but everything should have its limits. Be careful of the path you choose to follow and the energy you allow into your life. Changing the music you listen to or at least how music you listen to music, could be the start of something positive for you. You speak your reality into the universe when you constantly repeat these songs out loud. Now you think it's everyone else's fault but the entire time it's been you and what you accept into your life. You accept everything but the truth and that's a problem.

Unlearn what's been taught to you by your overprotective father. Keep your standards high but allow them to make sense by also having standards for yourself. You can't build with a man if you don't bring anything to the table. You are not the table! In the words of Ice Spice, "You think you the shit? You ain't even the fart". Don't be comfortable with a man building for you. Bring something to the project. Help build an empire. If it's just him building by himself then it lacks proper structure and that building will eventually fall.

Focus on reality; if most women are delusional, then this gives you an advantage to pass the competition by not being. Now you're ahead of the game and stepping on necks, and that sexy, that's something different, something special! So I ask you again, what's your something else?

So How Do You Fix It?

If anything in this chapter hit a nerve, good. That's a sign your spirit is tired of pretending. But don't just get mad. Get better. Delusion is a mindset. And like any mindset, it can be unlearned. Here are a few ways to start overcoming that princess complex and getting your mind right.

1. Ask Yourself the Hard Questions
   You want a certain type of man. Cool. But do you match him in value, mindset, and lifestyle? If the answer is no, work on it. Stop waiting to be rescued and start leveling up on your own. The best relationships are two whole people choosing to grow together, not one person carrying dead weight.

2. Get a Grip on Reality
   Your life is not a fairytale. Prince Charming is not riding in on a horse, and no, Michael B. Jordan is not about to pull up to your shift. Get real about your looks, your habits, your effort, and your expectations. This doesn't mean hate yourself. It means being honest. That's where growth starts.

3. Stop Comparing Yourself to Celebrities and IG Models
   They're entertainers. That's their job. Their bodies, money, and lifestyles are not your standard. Half of it is fake, edited, or bought. You will never have peace if you're constantly measuring yourself against a fantasy.

4. Practice Gratitude

Start saying thank you more often, even for the small stuff. Gratitude shifts your mindset from "I deserve everything" to "I'm grateful for what I have." That one change alone can open more doors for you than a big booty ever will.

5. Build Something for Yourself

Get your own. Stack your money. Learn a skill. Get fit. Read books. Challenge your thinking. That way, when a man does come along, he's an addition to your life, not your whole reason for existing.

6. Surround Yourself with Women Who Keep It Real

You need friends who check you, not cheer on your delusion. If your circle gasses up your fantasy world, it's time for a new circle. Get around people who live in the real world and hold each other accountable.

7. Get Comfortable Being Uncomfortable

Growth is not pretty. You're going to feel exposed, triggered, maybe even embarrassed. That's part of the process. Stay in it. Don't run. Be willing to sit in the truth until it changes you.

There's no shame in being wrong. The shame is in staying that way. You don't have to be delusional. You don't have to fake perfect. You don't have to live in fantasy. You can choose something better. You can choose to be real. That's where the real power is. And trust me, real is sexy.

Drive Is Attractive, A "Bad Bitch" Is Not

Who are you trying to be like? Beyoncé? Because Mrs. Carter is about to have yall self-proclaimed "Boss Bitches" old, single, and pretending to be happy. Why you would even want to be referred to as a "Bitch" anything is truly beyond me. You'll get mad if a man calls you one, yet you'll consistently refer to yourself as one. Please make it make sense. Do you think the meaning somehow changes when you say it? Do you feel less degraded because it came out of your mouth or your home girls?

It seems like you may have a confused outlook on what self-respect is supposed to look like. Most men have zero interest in a "Boss Bitch" or a "Bad Bitch" or a "Top Bitch" or a "HBIC" Or A "BITCH BITCH" outside of sex. Bitch anything really, unless it's a pitbull or husky. I mean why would they? All bitches do is piss everywhere and sniff their ass. They might as well get an expensive ass dog. It would be a lot less hassle than dealing with a human bitch of any kind.

Be Different

If your vocabulary is limited and you need better words to describe yourself and your qualities try words like Driven, Accomplished, or High Value. A man of high value will appreciate and respect these words and you a lot more instead of a title with the word "Bitch" in it. How do you want yourself to be seen? As A "Boss Bitch" or a Grown and Mature Woman who is Driven, Motivated, and has a plan? Don't do yourself dirty, don't sell yourself short, and don't eliminate an opportunity before you even get it. If you're going to advertise yourself, do it right. Use words that will get a man excited about building a future with you! Calling yourself a "Boss Bitch" could also give a man hint at the type of woman you are and the personality you may possess.

You have to speak to your dream man by advertising yourself as someone he would want to pursue a future with! Otherwise, you're just competing with other "Botton Bitches" for the best raggedy nigga you can get. Then ask God why this man treats you a certain way. When you call yourself a "Bitch" you only gonna attract a "Nigga", not a "Real Man of Value". Not a King that is gonna turn a princess into a Queen. A "Nigga" will

41

transform you from a "Boss Bitch" into a "Boss Bitch with another body", slowly decreasing your value to the man you want.

Mindset Is Everything

Just because you have your own everything, does not make you the woman the man you want is searching for. Mindset is everything. You gotta have enough knowledge to know and do better. Self-respect is important because a man will look at you as someone who can or cannot take care of his offspring and help build his household. It's not always about self-maintenance though yes that is important. A healthy humble mind tells a man more about you than painted nails and a lace front ever could. If you all have a daughter then he will consider how you will teach her and what personality traits will she get from you. Will you raise her to be a "Boss Bitch" or a strong driven woman who can take care of herself and her family? All of this matters. Those little qualities that you neglect are unfortunately for you what a "Good Man" is looking for. If you cannot display them then you turn into a stepping stone in any man's life. No man wants to marry a stepping stone, they just use it to get to the next stepping stone until eventually, the pathway leads him to the front door of his home. Be the home, not the stepping stone.

Don't be another piece of ass, don't be another baby momma. It's not like the world needs more of them anyway. A lot of women will get upset at a man for not wanting to date a woman with children, but if that man does not have kids and he spent his life managing the women in his life appropriately and valuing his body and who he choosing to lay down and have kids with then does that man not deserve a woman who was equality as responsible with her own body and soul? Does he not deserve to start his own family, versus adding to someone else's? In order to get the man you want, you need to become the woman that man is searching for.

Dressed for Attention, Crying for Respect

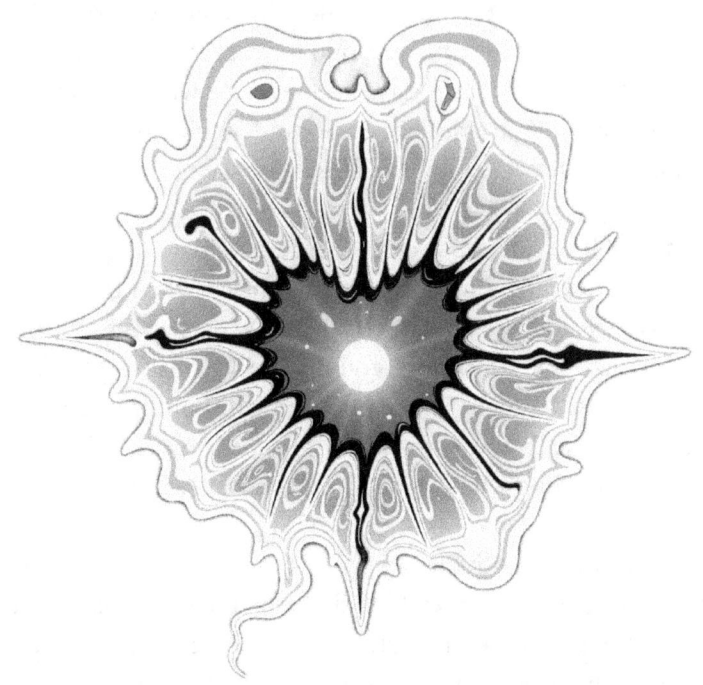

Nawwwww lets talk about this shit, if your outfit is saying one thing and your actions are saying another, don't be surprised when people believe what they see instead of what you say. The world don't run on excuses. You dress the part, you get treated accordingly. Simple as that. You can't step outside looking like a walking invitation and then catch an attitude when someone tries to RSVP. That's just how perception works.

If you put on a business suit, people assume you mean business. If you wear a bikini in the middle of the city, don't act brand new when people treat you like you're on vacation. If you're stepping out in a see-through dress with no bra and a thong, don't act like you don't understand why men are staring. It's not rocket science. People respond to what they see first, and your outfit is the first message you send. So why the fuck are so many women dressing one way and acting another, then crying about how nobody "understands" them?

Let's keep it real, if you want respect, dress like it. If you want attention, own it. But don't play confused when the world reacts to what you're putting out there. If you step into a room looking like sex, people are going to see sex before they see anything else. If that's what you want, cool. But if you're not about that life, then why the fuck dress like you are? This ain't about controlling women, it's about common sense.

And don't hit me with the "I wear this for me" argument. Cool, wear it for you. But understand that you don't live in a bubble. Your choices exist in a world full of people who will react accordingly. If you dress like a stripper, don't expect to be treated like a CEO. If you show up to a job interview in leggings and a crop top, don't be mad when they don't take you seriously. Perception is reality, and reality don't give a damn about your feelings.

You ever see a man dressed in a three-piece suit sagging his pants and throwing up gang signs? No, because men understand that presentation matters. If a man wears a Rolex and a tailored suit, you assume he's successful. If he's rocking slides with socks and a dirty wife beater, you assume he just rolled out of bed. It's the same logic. So why the hell do women act like they can dress however they want and still control the way the world perceives them?

And let's talk about social media. Some of y'all be half-naked in every post, then complain about men being thirsty in your DMs. Sis, the algorithm don't lie. If your page looks like an OnlyFans preview, don't be shocked when men assume you got a subscription link in your bio. If you want to attract quality men, you gotta present yourself as a quality woman. Ain't no way around it.

This ain't about telling women what to wear. It's about accountability. You want respect? Move like it. You want to be taken seriously? Present yourself accordingly. You can't scream "I'm a boss" while dressing like a backup dancer. You can't demand class while looking like you just got off the pole. And you damn sure can't cry about double standards while actively ignoring the ones that apply to everybody.

And while we're at it, let's talk about self-respect. Some of y'all think self-respect is just a buzzword you throw around when convenient. But real self-respect ain't about demanding respect from others, it's about carrying yourself in a way where you don't have to. It's about valuing yourself enough to understand that how you present yourself affects how people treat you. If you really respected yourself, you wouldn't feel the need to constantly put your body on display for validation. You wouldn't act one way in private but expect to be perceived differently in public. Self-respect is consistent. It doesn't change depending on the outfit you got on.

And let's clear up another delusion, this whole idea that men are the problem if they can't "control themselves" around a half-naked woman. Nobody's saying a man has the right to touch you just because you're showing skin. That's never okay. But acting like you can dress however you want with no reaction is just naive. Men are visual creatures. Always have been, always will be. You walk outside with your ass out, you will get attention. You can't sit here and act brand new like that's some shocking revelation. You don't put a steak in front of a dog and get mad when it starts drooling. That's just nature.

And let me hit you with a real-life example, something from my own past. Back in 1996, my mom took me to a Rainbow clothing store. I was just a baby, chilling in my stroller while she was checking out. Two young women in their 20s came up to me, calling me cute, pinching my cheeks, doing all that playful shit women do when they see a baby. And what did I do? I smiled and covered my eyes. Even laughed a little. They thought it was adorable and asked my mom, "Awww, why is he doing that?" My mom, without missing a beat, said, "Because he thinks you're naked." The girls laughed and walked away. But think about that. Even as an innocent baby, I had a natural understanding of modesty, of what was right and wrong, of what was moral and what was ill-moral.

So why the hell is it so hard for grown-ass women to grasp? The truth is, you don't want to. You like the attention, but you don't want to admit it. You enjoy turning men down, being rude, being dismissive, because it gives your little life some purpose. It makes you feel powerful. But you won't admit that either.

So here's the bottom line: your outfit should match your intentions. If you want respect, dress in a way that commands it. If you want attention, don't get mad when you get it. But don't mix the two and then act like the world is the problem when people react accordingly. Your look sets the tone before you even speak. Make sure the message you're sending is the one you actually want to deliver.

A lot of women will say they don't care how a man sees them, and that's cool, until they start complaining about the quality of men they attract. You can't have it both ways. If you truly don't care, then don't get mad when men treat you accordingly. But let's be real, most women *do* care. They just don't like admitting it because it forces them to take accountability for their own choices.

And that's the key here: accountability. If you're tired of the same type of men approaching you, maybe it's time to look at the energy you're putting out. It's not about changing who you are, it's about being honest with yourself. You say you want a man of value, a man who respects you, a man who sees you as more than just a body, but are you presenting yourself in a way that aligns with that?

That brings me to the next question: You might be out here searching for a certain kind of man, but is *he* searching for *you*? Because at the end of the day, attraction is a two-way street, and the type of man you *want* may not be looking for the type of woman you *are*.

A Girls Girl

Cut the shit, the term "a girl's girl" is a weapon. Y'all have taken a phrase that was supposed to be about female empowerment and twisted it into a hall pass for bad behavior. Being a girl's girl now means "I'm going to ride for women, even when they're dead wrong." That's not loyalty. That's delusion.

Somewhere along the line, this idea started getting used to justify some of the most toxic behavior I've ever seen. Women don't even need facts anymore. All they need is another woman saying "he did me wrong," and y'all ready to cancel, bash, or crucify that man without a second thought. You'll go to war for the wrong side just because they have a vagina.

Take Halle Bailey and DDG for example. Now before you start foaming at the mouth, let's just look at the facts. Halle is allegedly keeping their child away from DDG, not because he's abusive, not because he's a bad father, but simply because he doesn't want to be with her anymore. And yet, she's playing the victim card, lying publicly, dragging his name through the mud, involving courts and police, and weaponizing the system that was already designed to work against men.

And what do y'all do? You cheer her on. You excuse it. "Oh, she just had a baby," "It's postpartum," "He probably triggered her," "He's annoying anyway," like being annoying is grounds for getting stabbed or losing access to your kid? Seriously?

If the roles were reversed, and DDG was out here lying on Halle, keeping the baby from her, getting her caught up in legal mess just because she broke up with him, y'all would be outside with pitchforks calling for his head. But because it's a woman doing it, it becomes a "mental health struggle." Suddenly y'all are psychologists, lawyers, and trauma experts overnight, pulling excuses out of thin air just to keep her image clean. Oh, and did you hear? She dropped all the charges! Now why on earth would she do that? I wish I could put emojis in a book... Believe women? I would love to but look at your leaders.

Let me ask you this. When did "sisterhood" become more important than the truth? When did loyalty to gender replace loyalty to facts? Because what I see is a lot of women using "I'm a girl's girl" as a shield. You throw rocks, hide your hands, then cry victim while the other women surround you in a circle of protection no matter what damage you've done. It's honestly sad.

You're not a girl's girl. You're Satan's girl. You're enabling pain, division, and lies, and then dressing it up as empowerment. It's dangerous. And worse, it's teaching the next generation of women that accountability doesn't apply if you've got a group chat backing you up. But here's the thing. I'm not just here to bash. I'm here to help you think.

Let's flip the script for a second. What if the man being lied on, dragged through the courts, or denied access to his kid was your son? Would you still say "believe all women"? Would you still back a woman just because she's crying on Instagram or dropping cryptic captions? Or would you suddenly want the system to be fair? Would you demand truth, evidence, and accountability? Because I guarantee you, half of the stuff y'all cosign now wouldn't fly if it was happening to someone you raised, loved, or gave birth to.

And let's really talk about that for a second. Most women know how they raised their child. So when someone says, "Your son did this," a lot of y'all immediately feel something in your spirit because you know your son wouldn't even move like that. You know his character because you shaped it. Which brings up an uncomfortable truth. If you hate men so much because of how they act, ask yourself this. Who raised them?

If you're saying men are the problem but men weren't even around to raise them, then who are you really blaming? The answer is right there. Women raised these so-called toxic men. So how can you claim to be a girl's girl when you don't even respect what girls produce? You don't like men but you raised them. That's self-hate in disguise. If you don't like what came from you, then maybe the problem isn't just the men. It's what we keep choosing to ignore in ourselves.

And let me take it one step deeper. As a woman, have you ever cried just to get the reaction you wanted even though you knew you were wrong? Be real. If you're aware you've done this, then you must be aware that other women do it too. So why do you ignore it? Why act like women are always innocent when you know some women manipulate situations with tears, lies, or victimhood? Wouldn't the world be easier if men and women worked together instead of women acting like men are the enemy? Y'all walk around with these crazy unrealistic expectations, talking about you want the "three sixes": six figure income, six feet tall, and six pack abs. I ain't never seen a 6 foot stud with a six pack making six figures, yet studs always got a girl. Ain't that sad? You overlook regular hardworking men for a fantasy that doesn't even exist in your own community.

I Want To Help

So here's what you can do if you want to break out of this toxic girl's girl mindset:

1. Start with Truth, Not Emotion

It's easy to side with someone who feels right. But feelings don't equal facts. Learn to sit back, observe, and ask "What actually happened?" Not "Who do I like more?" Imagine how many men's lives could've been saved from false accusations if people paused to ask for evidence first. Careers destroyed. Reputations ruined. All because someone hit "share" or "like" without asking, 'Is this even true?' When you lead with feelings instead of facts, you don't just hurt one person, you contribute to a culture that treats unverified claims like gospel. That's not justice. That's emotional warfare.

2. Hold Women Accountable
Stop being scared to call your friend out. If she's wrong, she's wrong. Accountability isn't hate. It's love. Real friends don't let each other ruin lives or play victim for clout.

3. Think Before You React
If you see a video, post, or clip that triggers your emotions, pause before you repost or react. Ask yourself, "What if the person being accused was my brother, father, or son?"

4. Unlearn Blind Loyalty
Loyalty should be earned by character, not gender. Stop believing that being a woman makes someone inherently more honest or more right. It doesn't. We've all got flaws, and yes, some women lie too.

5. Prioritize Fairness Over Feminism
Not everything is about being a woman. Sometimes it's about being a decent human. Support women when they're right, but be brave enough to admit when they're wrong. Being a real one means standing on truth, not trends. And if you really want to help women grow, stop letting them hide behind the title "girl's girl" when what they really need is to grow the hell up.

Accountability is love. Fairness is power. And being honest about our flaws? That's real empowerment. Calling a 300-pound woman beautiful is delusion and enabling. Let's do better.

The Power of Vulnerability

Women love to scream about how they want a "real man," someone who's emotionally available, open, and communicative. But when the tables turn and it's their turn to be vulnerable? Silence. Women avoid vulnerability like it's the plague because deep down, they think it makes them look weak. They've been conditioned to believe that showing emotion means losing power, when in reality, the exact opposite is true.

You know what's actually weak? Walking around like you don't give a fuck when deep down, you care more than anybody. Acting like you're too independent for love, too "unbothered" to have real feelings, too strong to ever need anybody. That shit is fake. And not only is it fake, but it's hurting you more than you realize.

So let's talk about it. Because until you learn how to be vulnerable, you're going to keep attracting emotionally unavailable men, feeling disconnected in your relationships, and wondering why nobody ever truly sees *you*.

What Vulnerability Really Is (And What It's Not)

First off, let's get one thing straight: vulnerability is not the same as being weak, needy, or overly emotional. It's not about trauma dumping on a man on the first date or crying every time things don't go your way. Real vulnerability is about being *real*, being honest about your thoughts, your fears, your emotions, and trusting the right people with that information. What does that look like in real life? It's saying "I really like you" instead of playing dumb games. It's admitting "I'm scared of getting hurt" instead of pretending you don't care. It's being able to tell your partner, "I need reassurance sometimes," instead of pushing them away when they get too close.

What vulnerability *isn't* is acting reckless with your emotions. It's not about trauma bonding, using your pain for sympathy, or expecting people to fix you. There's a difference between being emotionally open and being emotionally unstable. You gotta know the difference.

The Fear of Being Seen (And Why That's a Good Thing)

Most women are scared of being truly seen. I don't mean seen like posting thirst traps on Instagram, I mean really *seen* for who they are without the filters, the walls, and the fake-ass "I'm fine" act. Because when you allow someone to see the real you, there's always a chance they won't like what they find. And that's terrifying, right?

But here's the thing: *you can't have real love or deep connections without vulnerability.* You can't expect a man to open up to you if you're too busy pretending you don't have emotions. Men connect with women who are *real*, not women who act like they have it all figured out.

Think about it. Who do you feel closer to: the friend who always acts perfect and never shares anything real, or the one who's honest about their struggles, their wins, and their fuck-ups? Exactly. The same goes for relationships.

How Avoiding Vulnerability Leads to Toxic Patterns

A lot of women claim they want a good man but then turn around and do everything in their power to push him away. Why? Because being vulnerable means giving someone the power to hurt you, and that's too scary for most people. So instead, they build walls. They play games. They sabotage shit before it even has a chance to get real.

Sound familiar? Ever caught yourself doing any of this:

- Ghosting instead of having an actual conversation about your feelings.
- Acting "too cool to care" even when you're literally obsessing over a text.
- Testing a man instead of communicating what you need.
- Pretending to be emotionless to protect yourself from getting hurt.

This kind of shit doesn't make you powerful. It makes you emotionally unavailable. And emotional unavailability only attracts more emotional unavailability. You ever notice how you keep getting dudes who are inconsistent, cold, or just don't take you seriously? Yeah. That's not a coincidence.

The Power of Vulnerability in Dating & Relationships

Here's the truth: Men respect women who are emotionally open. Not clingy, not reckless, but open. When a woman can confidently say what she wants, what she needs, and how she feels, it commands respect. Because it shows she's real.

Men actually *want* a woman they can trust, someone who makes them feel safe to open up too. But if you're over here acting like a robot, shutting down every real conversation, and running at the first sign of emotional depth, don't be surprised when the only men you attract are just as emotionally unavailable as you are.

Vulnerability isn't about "catching feelings too fast" or "letting your guard down too soon." It's about creating a relationship where both people feel safe to *be themselves.* If you want a man to truly connect with you, you have to be willing to *let him in.*

Practical Steps to Embrace Vulnerability

Alright, so how do you actually start being more vulnerable without feeling like you're throwing yourself to the wolves? Here's how:

1. **Figure out what you're afraid of.** Ask yourself: *Why do I struggle with vulnerability?* Is it fear of rejection? Fear of being hurt? Identifying your fear is the first step to overcoming it.
2. **Start small.** You don't have to spill your entire life story, but practice being honest in little ways. Express appreciation, admit when you're wrong, and communicate how you feel without overthinking it.
3. **Choose the right people.** Not everyone deserves your vulnerability. Being open doesn't mean trusting just *anybody* with your emotions. Pay attention to how people respond, if someone consistently dismisses your feelings, they're not the one.
4. **Reframe vulnerability as strength.** Every time you're real with someone, you gain power. Hiding your emotions isn't strength, it's fear. Confidence comes from owning who you are and not being afraid to show it.

Owning Your Power

The biggest lie women believe is that being vulnerable makes them weak. But the truth is, avoiding vulnerability is what's really holding you back. The strongest, most confident women are the ones who aren't afraid to be real. To say what they mean. To express what they feel. To actually *give a fuck* without fear of looking soft.

So if you've been out here playing the "I don't need nobody" game, ask yourself: *Is that really working for you?* Because if it was, you wouldn't be reading this right now. Try being vulnerable. Just once. See what happens. Bet on your relationship and your whole life change for the better.

Emotional Baggage Is Annoying

Okay, I can admit these chapter titles are a little harsh, but like I've already told you, I'm not here to spare feelings. I'm here to make you think, and I'm here to spark a want for change within you. I want you to understand that if you keep jumping from guy to guy, the chances of you being the actual problem are pretty high. I'd like to give you an analogy that I hope resonates with you.

Stinks Ova Here

I call this short story "Stinks Ova Here." It goes like this: There was a small boy from the deep south named Jimmy Bucket. Now Jimmy was getting ready for his first day of school; he was already super excited. Jimmy brushed his teeth and slicked his hair back, then made his way out the door; he didn't even grab breakfast. Jimmy quickly makes it to class, and he's paying close attention to the teacher talking; suddenly, little Jimmy smells something. "Sniff, sniff, sniff, eww," Jimmy says to himself.

Soon after, Jimmy's hand goes right up, and he yells loud enough for the entire class to hear him, "TEACHER!! STINKS OVA HEAR!!!" The teacher calmly responds to him as the class laughs at the outburst, "Well, Mr. Bucket, what do you think it is?" Without hesitation, Jimmy pointed to little Miss Sarah, sitting at the desk beside him, and said, "Well, I... I Think it's this girl next to me". Sarah then begins to cry, clearly hurt by the accusation. So the teacher then says, "Okay, Jimmy, let's move your seat." Jimmy then responds with a loud "Thaannnkkk Yooouu!" Not even caring that he hurt little Miss Sarah's feelings. He gathered his materials, and he moved from the front of the class to the middle of the class.

A few minutes later, "sniff sniff sniff sniff," Jimmy's hand shoots up again, and without even waiting for the teacher to call on him, he says, "Teacher! Stinks Ova Here Too, and it's gotta be the boy next to me." The teacher responds, "Okay, Mister Buckett, let's move you again." Jimmy then packed his things and moved to the last row of the class. At the same time, he is smelling the air, saying, "Yeah, this is much better." In response, the teacher says, "Good, I'm glad now. Please try and pay attention".

Some time goes by, and Little Jimmy starts sniffing again! "Sniff, Sniff." Jimmy lets out a big loud "EWWWWW" and, without even raising his hand with the same vocal tone, yells, "TEACHA STANKS OVA HERE TUU! AND I THINK IT'S BARBRA NEXT TO ME." Now Barbra, the little girl sitting on the same row next to him, begins to cry. The entire class is looking back, giving Jimmy real nasty glares, but he doesn't care. He yells out to the class, "DONT LOOK AT ME LIKE THAT! YALL SHOULDNT COME TO SCHOOL STANKING!" Now the teacher steps in and says, "Okay enough, Mister Bucket, how about we sit you in the corner by yourself." Jimmy says with a grin, "Fine by me." Now, Little Jimmy Buckett is sitting alone, smiling, taking notes.

"Sniff, Sniff, ohh nooo," Jimmy says to himself. He slowly raises his hand once again. "Yes, Jimmy," The teacher says calmly. The class then turns around and looks at the now embarrassed Little Jimmy Buckett. "Teacher, it stinks over here." At that moment, the class begins to laugh at Jimmy. "Shhhh," Says the teacher, "Well, Mister Buckett, maybe it's you. Do you have something on you?" Jimmy starts sniffing; he sniffs the air, puts his head down, and touches his hair. He smells his hand. The class begins to laugh once again as Jimmy gags from the stench.

It turns out that back in the day, especially in the Deep South, where Jimmy is from, folks would use lard or bacon grease to style or slick their hair back. Usually, this would be fine, but today, unfortunately for Jimmy, his grease went bad. Imagine walking around with rancid bacon grease on top of your head.

So Jimmy went all around that classroom hurting feelings,

making enemies, and spreading his funk, thinking it had to be any and everybody else besides him while also assuming that moving on to the next situation would solve the real problem.

Moral Of The Story

What was the moral of this story? If you said not to put cooking products in your hair after they expire, then you are correct! I'm playing, not really, though that isn't a bad takeaway. The actual moral of this story is, drum roll, please…. SOMETIMES IT'S YOU!

Now, here is the truth for you: story time is over! If you carry emotional baggage, you must understand that most men who are worth something have no interest in shouldering that. Don't get me wrong, we all get scared up over the years, but adults who agonize at the thought of intimacy, and I'm not talking about sexual intimacy. I'm talking about the women who will open their legs before they open their hearts.

Women that will play the blame game or leave because it's the easiest thing to do. They are disconnected emotionally and allow their past traumas to guide them. They often refuse to listen to reason, lean upon their own understanding, and do not seek the proper guidance to build themselves up to be able to maintain a healthy relationship. These women are not worth the risk, even to the men out there who are Captain Saveahoes.

Women who jump from man to man or relationship to relationship, thinking it's always the other person, they're dangerous. That also brings us back to accountability. You being scared to open up or making a man wait to receive the love he's already proven he deserves due to nothing, but your mental state or traumas will get you nothing but a higher body count!

The Unsettling Truth

A lot of people think settling just means ending up with an ugly motherfucker or a broke one, but that ain't even the half of it. Settling is when you accept less than what you actually want or deserve just because you're tired of waiting, scared of being alone, or convinced you can't do better. It's dating someone who doesn't really make you happy but "checks some boxes." It's staying in a relationship where you feel unfulfilled because you've convinced yourself this is the best you're gonna get.

It's tolerating bullshit ,disrespect, inconsistency and lack of ambition, because you don't want to start over. And let's be real, most people settle all the damn time. They just call it "being realistic" or "compromising," but really, it's just fear dressed up as logic. The worst part? Once you settle, you get stuck. You tell yourself, "This is fine," but deep down, you know it's not. Years pass, and before you know it, you're looking at your partner, thinking, "How the hell did I get here?"

Signs You're Settling

Not sure if you're settling? Here's how you know:

1. **You make excuses for them constantly.** If you find yourself always justifying their actions, "He's just stressed," "She's going through a lot," "It's not that bad", then yeah, you're probably settling.
2. **You feel more drained than fulfilled.** A good relationship should add to your life, not take from it. If you're constantly frustrated, sad, or bored, that's a sign.
3. **You've stopped trying to improve the relationship.** If you've mentally checked out and are just going through the motions, you already know you're not happy.
4. **You're scared of starting over.** The only reason you're staying is because the idea of being single sounds worse than the reality of your relationship.
5. **You don't actually admire or respect them.** Attraction fades, but respect and admiration are what keep things solid. If you don't genuinely look up to your partner in some way, you're settling.
6. **You're more in love with their potential than who

they actually are. You keep telling yourself, "One day they'll change," but deep down, you know they won't.

7. **Your gut is screaming at you, but you keep ignoring it.** Your intuition is loud as hell, but you just keep shushing it because you don't want to deal with the truth.

Why Do People Settle?

Settling usually comes from a place of fear and scarcity. People convince themselves they won't find someone better, that they're too old, that dating is too exhausting, or that love is just about "choosing someone and making it work."

Society also doesn't help. Women especially get hit with this pressure to lock someone down before a certain age, as if being single at 30 is some kind of death sentence. That's how people end up marrying partners they're not even excited about, then waking up years later wondering why they feel so fucking empty.

Then there's the comfort factor. People get used to what's familiar. Even if it's shitty, at least they know what to expect. Starting over is scary. Learning someone new is exhausting. So they stay put, convincing themselves it's not *that* bad.

Let's not forget the way society gaslights people into thinking love is *supposed* to be hard. Struggle love is glorified, like it's some noble thing to endure a bunch of bullshit before you "earn" a good relationship. People settle because they think *that's just how it works.* They see their parents, their friends, movies, and they internalize the idea that being miserable is just part of the package.

But let me ask you this: if you're doing all this work to keep a relationship going, but your partner ain't putting in the same effort, are you really in a relationship? Or are you just in an unpaid internship?

How to Avoid Settling

If you don't want to wake up in 10 years resenting your partner (or worse, yourself), here's what you need to do:

Know Your Non-Negotiables. Before you even start dating seriously, get clear on what actually matters to you. If ambition, emotional availability, or sexual compatibility are must-haves, don't talk yourself into accepting less.

Stop Worrying About What Other People Think. Your friends, your mom, society—none of them have to live your life. If you're staying in a relationship because it looks good instead of because it feels right, you're already making the wrong choice.

Develop a Mindset of Abundance. The idea that "good men/women are hard to find" is bullshit. The world is full of people who will match your energy. But if you believe there's no one better out there, you'll act like it—and that's how people end up stuck with the wrong person.

Learn to Be Okay Alone. The easiest way to stop settling is to not need a relationship in the first place. When you're genuinely happy on your own, you won't tolerate half-assed love just to fill a void.

Pay Attention to How You Feel. If deep down, something always feels off, trust that. Your body and mind know when you're lying to yourself.

Date With Intention. Stop dating just because you're lonely. Date because you actually want a connection, and be intentional about who you entertain.

Be Willing to Walk Away. If you're afraid to leave, you're already in too deep. Walking away from the wrong situation is the only way you'll ever make space for the right one.

The Cost of Settling

Settling doesn't just rob you of happiness, it steals years of your life. Years that you could've spent building something real with someone you actually want. Years that you could've spent finding yourself instead of trying to make something work that was never meant to.

Settling leads to resentment. And resentment festers. It turns into bitterness, regret, and sometimes even hatred. Next thing you know, you're looking at your partner with disgust, realizing that you gave up on yourself the moment you chose them.

And let's talk about the long-term effects. Settling in relationships usually spills over into the rest of your life. When you lower your standards in love, you start lowering them everywhere else. You stop pushing for the career you want. You tolerate friendships that drain you. You accept less because you've convinced yourself you don't deserve more.

Settling is easy. It's comfortable. It's safe. But safe doesn't mean right. And if you've ever had that gut feeling that you deserve more, you probably do. The sooner you admit that to yourself, the sooner you can go get what you actually want.

Because the truth is, you don't just wake up one day happy in a relationship you settled for. You wake up with regret. And trust me, regret is a hell of a lot harder to live with than being single.

If you take nothing else from this chapter, take this: you owe it to yourself to want more. To expect more. To *demand* more. The second you start acting like you deserve better, watch how fast your life changes. And don't let anyone, family, friends, or society, convince you otherwise. Work hard for what you want, unlearn bad habits and become who you need to be to attract who you truly want.

Having A Baby Decreases Your Value

Oh, y'all all finna hate me for this one. That's one hell of a chapter title, isn't it? You find that to be a common theme throughout this book. Think about what I'm saying for a second though. Let's break it down, shall we? Am I saying having a baby decreases your value as a person? Absolutely not! We are all equal...kind of... Anyway, I'm saying it decreases your marital market value. So if you're not looking to get married then this chapter isn't for you, go ahead and skip it. Actually, just put the entire book down. Because the truth is if you're not ready for marriage you're honestly not even ready to date. Otherwise, you're dating for what reason? To have fun? Vlad Savchuk once said if you wanna have fun go get a dog or a hobby, You don't use another person's heart for fun. So if you're interested in finding a mate, pay attention.

A Truth

Men don't care to raise another man's kids, they would rather raise their own. This is a fact! Now yes, some men are willing to do that. This is true; however, I promise you that there are reasons for it. For instance, that woman may be that man's first love, and he hasn't learned the life lesson of dating a single mother yet. Maybe that man has decided for himself that he doesn't want kids of his own and is okay with never having the full responsibility of being that child's father. may have some really good pussy. That woman may also do her part in making that man feel superior, making him feel as though he matters. A lot of single mothers have that problem, especially if they have sons. They get weird. Either way, that woman provides something the average woman with a kid does not. Maybe she has some really good pussy. Maybe she read my book and made the proper changes. Who knows!

All I'm saying is that man does not naturally love that child like he would his own, not right off the back. He may grow to love the child, but it's whatever the mother is providing that makes him even offer the attempt. It starts with something else first, then the love begins. What is your something else? If you have kids already you gotta find it. Having some good pussy might be good enough to get a man but will never be good enough to keep one.

Plus if he stays around you want him to be loyal right? How loyal can a man who is motivated by sex really be? If his main reason for being you is you have some good pussy, then all is for some new good pussy to come along and he'll be disloyal to you. A man who's motivated by sex has a higher likelihood of cheating.

Now what do you think about what you just read? Did any of this upset you? I hope not because this was a logical statement. Don't allow yourself to think with your emotions. Instead, use your reasoning skills and reread the beginning of the chapter so you may truly take in what I'm saying to you.

Too Many Damn Kids

The more kids you have the more your value decreases. I knew a beautiful woman who had a lot of money, and all she wanted to do was spend it on me, but she had five kids and three baby daddies. I just couldn't! I don't date for fun so if I stay with her knowing I would never want to marry her because of all them damn kids Id be playing around, dating for fun, using her.

Think of it on a scale from 1 to 10. Everyone wants to be a 10, but how on earth can you be a 10 when you're walking around here with multiple kids? Even worse, if you have multiple baby fathers. You can't seriously think you're a 10; if you do, you're delusional. Having kids by multiple men shows other men that you did not value your body in your younger years. It brings up trust issues and creates a lack of respect.

Why would you expect a man to place value on your body if

you didn't? You just walking around letting niggas nut inside of you. At least that's what that man is gonna think. All you've done is show that man two things. Number 1, all you're good for is sex. Number 2, make sure you use protection because you are most definitely gonna keep it. That makes your extra fertile ass dangerous! Probably try to get him for child support. Men don't trust shit like that, you can't even blame them. Even if you're not like that, there are so many women out here that are, men just proceed with caution.

How The Scale Works

Okay so back to the scale. Remember 1 To 10. You're absolutely gorgeous, a straight 10 on the scale, with no physical flaws, right? Well if you got three kids now you're a 7. That's only if they all have the same father. That shows a man that maybe you were in a long-term relationship, and it didn't work out for whatever reason. Though that might still bring up some red flags, a man would more likely be interested in this woman than a woman with three kids and two baby fathers. If you were a 10 and you have three kids and two baby fathers now you're a 5. Is the math starting to make sense to you now?

Now, how do you overcome this obstacle if you already have kids? Is it possible to increase your ranking on the scale after having a bunch of kids? Yes, it is! You must add value to yourself. That brings us right back to the repeating question of the book. What is your something else?

High Body Counts Are Disgusting

Let's be honest, I'm not telling you anything you don't already know. Of course, it's a fact that we live in a society today that pushes the "My Body My Choice" narrative. Though yes I do slightly agree with that concept, I also feel like it's the excuse women have given themselves to go be whores and sleep with as many people as they want to. Then, they may be confused about why they can't keep a man. Even have a certain delusion within them that her little wide open pussy still hit the same when lord knows it ain't hit the same since you were 20 years old. Being 20 years old with 10-plus bodies on your resume is crazy and disgusting. What man do you think wants that?

Let's Take It Back

Let's talk real quick, shall we? Do you remember your first love? That is if you ever had one. I'm sure most of us have. How did you feel about him? How many men have you felt that way about since then? How many sexual partners have you had since him? Was he among your first 5 sexual experiences? Was he in the top 3? Was He the best? How long did he hold that title? Did you enjoy sex with him the most because of the love you shared? These are all questions I want you to ask yourself.

Women are emotionally driven creatures. The more partners you add to your body count the harder it will be to connect emotionally to a man. Not being able to connect emotionally with your partner will surely create problems down the line. It will even make it harder to bond with each other.

Even worst is a woman that believes she can connect easily with any man she fucks. This is a dangerous woman. I'm not saying you have to be a virgin, having 7 or 8 bodies before you are even 21 is not attractive. Having 3 is a better number but more than that will tell a man what your priorities are, and your maturity level. It tells me that you don't value your own body and you don't have self-control. It also tells me that your parents let you do what you want or they weren't there. Which also tells me you come from a questionable home. Which lets me know this isn't a woman I want to raise my children. This leads to me still fucking you but never marrying you and the next thing you know you just added another body to your resume.

Double Standards A Real

Here's another truth most women hate to hear. A woman that has sex with a lot of men is a slut, but a man that has sex with a lot of women is a slut maker. Double standards are very real, but that is the world we live in. If you move to Canada it will be the same thing. If you move to China it will be the same thing. If you move to India it will be the same thing. If you move to a foreign country you might not even have a choice in who you get to have sex with.

I know Meghan The Stallion is messing these young girls' heads up. Honestly, she ruins their chances of finding good men. Most men look for a pure wife. Someone who has taken care of their body and not given everyone access to it. Most women look for a man who has already begun to establish his empire and now needs a queen. You have some women and men that look to build with each other as well. Those are my favorite types of relationships!

Think about this for a second. Why would a King make a Queen out of a woman all the village men are fucking? That's not sacred, that's not attractive, it's embarrassing and disgusting to him. Those men turn that woman into a slut, and a slut cannot be a Queen, no matter what delusion you wanna convince yourself of. So don't walk around concerning yourself with the double standard, because that's not going anywhere. You can have all the protests you want. This was how it's been since before you and it will be the same long after you're dead and gone.

If you want a man who doesn't have a lot of bodies, that's perfectly fine, too. Go search for him and when you find him, submit yourself to him. Do all you can to make that relationship work, not to keep him! There's a big difference between the two. Women will be quiet and learn their place, they will learn better habits like apologizing and submission, all to make the relationship work. Women will stalk you after they fucked up or trap you with a baby to keep you. Big difference. If you can't seem to find a man with a lower body count than the average man, that doesn't mean you should push the narrative that something is wrong with society. Don't fall for the trap that modern-day independent women set for you. These hoes are single because they can't keep a man, not because they don't want one. If you let them tell it it's by choice, and that may be true… Just not their choice.

Don't Fight Back, Just Leave!

I never understood the whole "scared to leave" concept. I most likely never will. If you're with a man and he is hurting you, beating you, abusing you, then get the heck away. You can't convince me you're staying for any other reason than stupidity. Please just make it make sense! He threatens to kill you if you leave, call the cops, and get a restraining order. Buy a gun and don't be afraid to use it on that mother fucker. Shoot his dumb ass if he violates that restraining order. Move states or even countries. There are way better places to live besides the USA anyway.

Do anything! Don't just stay like an idiot, but more importantly, don't try and fight back. Your best option is to run, leave, get the fuck outta there! If he is sexually abusive then again I say, kill his ass. You are protecting yourself and no human male or female deserves to go through something like that. Don't lie to yourself and say you're staying outta love, No you're staying because you're stupid. You are weak-minded and you weren't raised right. You were raised to be a pussy and to let people run over you and take advantage of you. You think you're showing respect or submissiveness by letting your partner physically harm you but you're showing weakness and a lack of self-love.

Consequences Behind The Actions

Unless a man is in a life-threatening position or is defending himself against someone trying to harm him, there is no reason for him to be hitting on a woman. Hitting a woman goes against our genetic makeup. If he hurts a woman for no reason other than to protect himself then he should serve that time in jail. However, if a man takes away the ability of a woman to choose, by raping her, he's breaking not only most government laws around the world but also breaching the laws of natural selection. He should be permanently put to sleep to protect the balance and integrity of the human species.

A woman who experiences either of these two life-changing tragedies but is willing to stay begins to forfeit her right to proper justice. Keep this in mind. Don't put yourself in a worse position because you think you are in love with a man who has proven that he doesn't love you, at least he doesn't love you enough to value your body. Even if you're married, that still does not give him the right to insert himself inside of you whenever he wants, completely disregarding your mood or feelings on the matter. That's called "Presumption of Intimacy" and though it is NOT the same as rape, it is a close cousin and should be addressed before dangerous unchangeable habits began to form.

Do Not Tempt A Man

This does not mean you're allowed to tempt that man to act surprised at their sexual arousal. We live in a world today where a woman can walk out in a public area dressed sexually provocatively and expect to still receive respect. If it looks like a duck quacks like a duck and walks like a duck then it's a duck. The same can be said for whores.

They put all men in a category but fail to realize they're surrounded by different cultures, mental health, addictions, predators, and criminals. These men are not expected to follow the same rules as our standard society. So I urge you ladies to be careful with not only your public appearance but also your mindset. Thinking that you are untouchable or you can beat a man is dangerous. Personally, I will fuck you up if you put your hands on me, and I know for a fact you can't be me, unfortunately, you've somehow convinced yourself that you can, and that's gonna get you fucked up. Don't even act like you wanna put your hands on me. I will give you chances but no adult human is about to just put their hands on me violently and think that it's acceptable. You're better off walking away.

If you got your ass out in public and you see me looking at it.

You better not say shit rude to me, your ass is out. You don't want people to look at it and then put your ass away. Don't tempt a man. Don't dangle nectar in front of a species that is known for being unpredictable. Don't be the "Forbidden Fruit". Because Adam took a bite of that fruit even though he knew the consequences.

A man will know the negative reaction to his actions but if the desire is strong enough he will easily say fuck it. Don't make yourself a target and then cry victim when something happens, regardless of how YOU believe society to act! Don't put your own morals and values on other people then be surprised when they don't fall in line with your mindset. It doesn't make them right for their choices, but it doesn't make you right either. Just because you say they shouldn't doesn't mean they won't.

Use Your Brain

You must be smart when it comes to accessing the situation. This means choosing your battles wisely. Sometimes it is smarter to retreat so that you may live to fight another day. If a man is hitting or beating you, figure out why it's happening. Does he have anger issues, drug problems, or alcohol addiction, was he abused growing up? Maybe he's just a dick. You may want to also consider other options that may require you to take accountability. Did you say or do something? Did you hit him first? If so then why are you surprised that you got hit back?

Men nowadays are not raised to not hit women, yet they are raised to defend themselves. I remember being a kid. While growing up my mother used to tell me not to let any woman put their hands on me and to defend myself. So yes I say this again, if a woman hits me or harms me, ima smack the lace front off her head. I will not beat on a woman though.

Ladies, my final tip on this subject is simply this, don't beg a man all day to hit you and then play the victim role when he does. Don't even be surprised, don't cry to call the cops, don't call your brother or your ex, and don't call him crazy. Take that shit because you asked for it. Again, I'm not saying he is right, but I am saying that whether or not he is right or wrong is not gonna stop you from getting fucked up. We are talking about common sense and survival. Just leave and think about the part you played in the situation so you may avoid it in the future.

Trust me when I say a lawyer repeating your words in court will not look good and you will lose that case. Just think about it. "Your Honor the so-called victim's exact words were "I wish you would hit me, hit me I dare you, I want you to, please hit me" My client simply gave her what she asked for." Do you see my point ladies? There are plenty of dudes out here granting wishes. My advice to you, be careful what you wish for!

Lady In The Streets, But A...

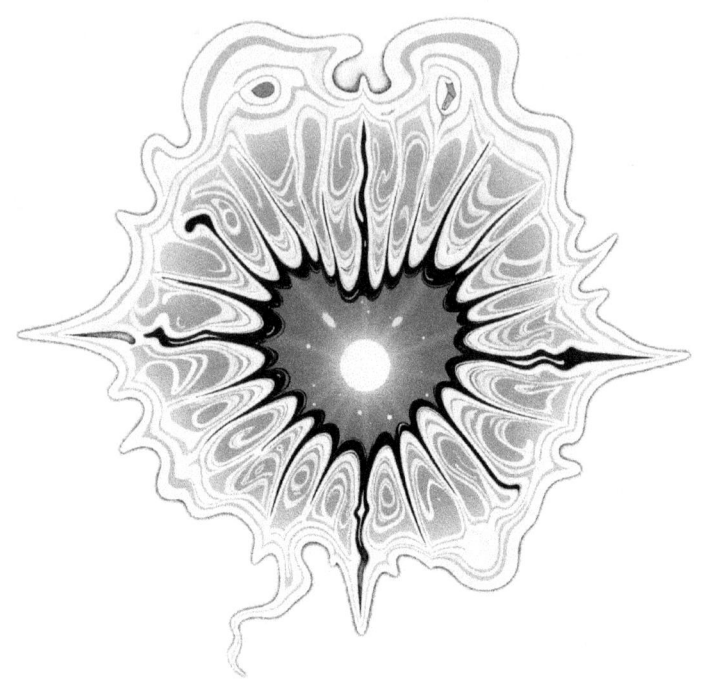

Come on, you know the rest of it! We want a lady in the streets but a freak in the sheets! If you're more urban you might say bed. Shout out to Ludacris! This should be self-explanatory but if it's not, don't trip. I got you! There are plenty of things a woman can do that a man will absolutely hate, but on the very top of that list is being a hoe! I'll make it easy for you to understand. No man wants another man to know how his woman's body looks or feels. They certainly don't want another man to know what she does in an intimate setting.

That should be reserved for her man and her man only! There

is a time and a place for everything. "In the sheets" does not necessarily mean at home, or in the bed. It more so refers to the privacy of your relationship. So if you are the freaky type, the type that likes Mall bathrooms or empty movie theaters, and randomly get it on with your partner, then that's your right!

Flaunting your body around and speaking dirty while in the presence of other people, especially other men is an entirely different story. Being a lady in the streets is kinda like having a secret identity. Like Superman or Wonder Woman, but only your man knows what's underneath your disguise. He's the only one who knows how nasty you can get for him, and that's how it should be!

Is This Even For You?

Showing off what your man got to the world should make you feel like you are not just for him. Why would you want to be for anyone else other than your man? Remember that these tips are not for the everyday woman but for women looking to try a new way of life and find their forever person. They have been out in the streets already, and they're tired of them and are ready to find a healthy stable home. They realized that maybe how they already lived their life may be a contributing factor to the reason they are currently single and past relationships have been unsuccessful.

If I haven't described you then I'm not sure why you're still reading this book. If you're the woman who wants to wear panties to the gym and call them shorts or the woman who likes to go to Miami every summer with your friends and you don't want that to change then this book is not for you, and the advice I give may come off offensive or old fashioned. Your alternative is getting dressed in your most revealing outfit just to lie to yourself and the people around you by saying you do it for yourself and not for any man's attention. Get over yourself and grow up.

How To Reach Queen Status

Explore in your bed with your man, be silent in the presence of other men. Allow your man to feel like a man and take pride in it! Learn your role! Think about why American men leave the country to find their wives. Have you ever wondered why? It's because, in every country that's not America, the women are submissive, they are respectful, and they stay in their place not only in the relationship they are in but also as women. American men cannot get that here! Why don't you be that rare diamond! You be that something else.

Respect your man like a King and you will become a Queen. That's the only way to truly earn Queen status. Keep in mind that not all Queens are Queens. We call women Queens nowadays very loosely. Zero discipline with our tongues with that word. Especially my black sista's. We raise them to think they are already Queens, and yes in normal conversation I would refer to ALL black women, in fact, black people as a whole as Kings and Queens. I don't mean it in the same way I am currently referring to Queen status. The melanin in our skin and where we come from mixed with what we have gone through and survived as a culture makes us Kings and Queens, but how a woman treats her man and takes care of her family truly decides if she's worthy of that Queen status or not.

To be a true Queen you must also have a King. Here is a fact, a King can be a King without a Queen but a Queen cannot be a Queen without a King. It might also be a good idea to note that not all men are King Status so you would do yourself a great justice to choose wisely my dear sister. Sometimes, looks are not everything. Sometimes, the man who will not only turn you into a queen but also treat you like a queen might be under 6 feet tall, not have a beard, and live in his mom's basement. A king is not a king because of the quantity of his wallet but because of the quality of his heart!

Make The Right Choice

Choose a man who has spent his singleness building himself up to prepare for a Queen, because that will be the man who will be looking for the exact woman this book is teaching you to become. A woman with determination and goals. A woman with respect for herself and her man. Who values privacy and considers her body sacred to her partner. A woman who has either spent her single years building her worth and not destroying it or trying to make the changes needed to be what she needs to be to reach Queen's Status. A woman who has spent her time taking care of her body not sharing it or showing it.

These are the women who will inherit the gifts and blessings promised to them. These are the women who will become Queens and rule side by side with their King to rule over their household and start building their empire. Together, raising self-respecting Princes and Princesses to one day become self-respecting Kings and Queens to their future Queens and Kings. Breaking a cycle and continuing their legacy.

Can You Be Trusted?

There are a few good women in the world who will seriously ride for their man. Those are the types of women that truly hold their man down. They would go to jail for their man. They are on his side whether he is right or wrong. These women are also crazy, yet I respect them! I love what they stand for, a true ride or die! Then you got the opposite end of the spectrum. You got the woman who's an impulsive liar. She keeps no secrets and would lie on her man just to see him in handcuffs. This same woman will also cry directly in your face with a runny nose and swear she is telling the truth while knowing damn well she is lying. These are the same women that lie about being raped, or even getting shot in the foot. Free Tory Lanez. That man almost died over a woman's lie…

Who Can You Trust?

Women who crack under the pressure of their family and peers. You can't even trust her to tell the truth about what she had for breakfast this morning unless you are her gay best friend. Women who get caught in the lie then keep the lie up. Women who swear up and down you can trust them but even they know that you can't, but their goal isn't to build a trusting relationship, their goal is to manipulate you and the situation they're in with you until you're of no more use to them.

Like I said there are plenty of examples of women lying and crying at the same time right in their man's face. Don't be fooled! These women can shut these tears off quicker than a sink faucet. This is not the woman a good man would be searching for. Why would he want a woman like that in his household? How could he ever trust her if most of her personality is based on lies, deceit, and manipulation? What would she raise his kids to be like? Liar? Probably! Could he even trust her to raise the kids? Probably not! Might as well have a baby with a crackhead. It would be a similar outcome.

Think about it, would you want someone who is known for lying to watch over your kids? No? Okay, then why would you even have a child with them in the first place? You wouldn't! Why would you want that crazy ass DNA flowing through your child's body!

Be Careful

Women try to be so careful trying to make sure the man… wait… pause, now restart that sentence. Some women try to be careful trying to make sure the man they choose to have kids with is sound of mind, has no criminal background, has good parents and upbringing, has no mommy or daddy issues, and has no mental health problems. Unfortunately, they themselves have all of these same problems plus some. It may be difficult for some women.

They have been lying for so long they just can't help it at this point. It's like second nature for them to be dishonest. You may find it a struggle yourself, telling lies in moments you don't need to. Not that you should ever lie, but let's be honest and say some things people lie about are just plain stupid. Like why are you lying about certain shit? It just doesn't make any sense! Gotta be a form of impulse disorder.

I believe honesty is always the best policy in any situation. When you are honest, you develop a reputation for being a trustworthy person. When you are known as a trustworthy person, your relationship will become easier, especially communication, all before your very eyes. You'll be able to tell your partner something without them questioning whether or not you're being truthful with them.

Hell, you won't even have to look over your shoulder. Keeping up with lies you told, the stress of forgetting a lie you told, and then getting caught in it weeks or months later. I'm sure that will be a relief.

The sad truth about lying is that you can't just tell one lie and it's over with. You end up telling another one then another one then another one. You do all of this just to keep covering for the original lie you told, and before you know it, you are six lies deep and gotta remember every detail of each lie just to not get caught up. Now the consequences will be much greater because not only did you tell that first lie, but now you're lying back to back to try and save yourself. What type of person would you call someone like that?

That's way too much stress if you ask me. Why are you lying in the first place? Are you trying to avoid hurting someone's feelings? Even worse, are you trying to preserve your innocence? Neither is good, and both are immature. You are grown! At least you're supposed to be. If you did that shit own up to it! Don't be a pussy!

Honesty Is Always The Best Choice

By lying you begin to create negative energy as well as an unsafe environment for yourself and whomever you're trying to spare the hurtful truth from. You're also proving that the love you say you have for that individual is not real. Trying to spare yourself from the consequences or their reaction to the truth is not real love or self-love love. You have no interest in growing as a person and you are a scared little baby bitch.

You're digging yourself a hole with no later and sooner or later all the lies will begin to drown you. Your relationship will start to feel more like work, like waking up every morning to perform a job. Most people are excited to start a new job. What happens after they deal with the same bullshit every day for long periods of time? If you said get a raise then you're wrong! You will become miserable, but you late, because your partner was miserable before you. You just end up hating the job overall or hating the relationship.

Don't reach a point in your relationship where you're not even sure if you're telling the truth when you tell him you love him, because that can happen! Let that man go, let him find someone he can truly love and that won't waste his time. Someone who means it when they tell him they love it, someone who won't lie to him and hurt him just because they are not able to manage their own emotions and reactions. Spare both of you the pain you're about to cause or have been causing. Have enough respect for yourself and your partner to tell them the truth, even when it seems the most difficult to do so. So what if the truth hurts! The truth will set you free!

The truth will gain you respect, plus no one ever said it would be easy. Remember this, men are dumb, but they are not stupid. Meaning yes, we do dumb shit like get an injury and decide to sleep it off instead of going to the hospital. But we also know when something is up in our relationship, even if we don't always comment on the things we see, hear, and feel. It's not like ya'll women do the best job at hiding your emotions. Especially you ladies with "tells". Like pulling your hair out, stress eating, or the woman who can't hide her facial expressions.

We as men notice things sometimes and will never say a word. Some men look for you to come back with the truth, giving you the chance to redeem yourself. This man has a tremendous amount of patience. If you're one of these women who lie like an old rug then I'm sorry to tell you you're going to have a stressful and lonely life!

Using A Man Is Dangerous

It's only fitting that I let you know that some of these men out here will seriously kill you! There's a large group of men who have mental health problems that they are not even aware of until they come across the right or in this case the wrong woman. There are men out there who are good guys and have the purest of intentions. Men who are rescuers by nature.

Evil Women

Unfortunately, there are also women out there who will take that same good man and abuse him, take advantage of him.

These women receive some form of joy from hurting a good man. They will take his heart and every other fiber of his being and crush it into the most brittle, rigid, fragile ball they can turn it into without a care in the world or a concern for the pain or damage they've just caused.

They will lie and tell them they love them. They'll move in with him and live off of him. They take full advantage of the security and stability that he provides for them. All the while never fully committing themselves to him. Taking all the birthday gifts, Christmas gifts, vacations. All the flowers, blood, sweat, real tears, support, and memories. Taking a piece of him as he falls deeper in love with her. After she's done taking and taking and taking she will take all her gifts, memories, and his happiness and disappear into the night without a care in the world. Leaving this man with nothing but pain and confusion.

Damaged Men

Now this damaged man will go off and enter his subsequent relationship with a guard up. He will move in a specific way to prevent him from feeling that same pain ever again. He may have met himself a good woman, but he can't tell because he thought the last one was a good woman. Now he can't trust his judgment and his way of solving the problem is to treat all women the same. Now that good woman he met is catching the short end of the stick. She truly loves him, but he can be an asshole at times.

For all the things he did in that last relationship, he swore to the universe that he would never give another woman that side of him again. Now, the new woman leaves and treats the next man she is in a relationship with just as badly. She also goes on for the rest of her life, thinking that all men are dogs. Women will stay in a relationship with a man knowing she never wanted to be with him but didn't want to leave the comfort he provided her. They don't want to lose the benefits. Some are in a relationship with a person they know they will never say yes to marrying simply because they don't want to be single.

Some know they got a good man and don't want another woman to have him so they stay, and become bitter. They begin to plot, flirt with coworkers, talk to ex-boyfriends, give their number out, and then use the excuse of friendship as if we were all in middle school. Hoping and praying the man they are with turns out to be just as much of a dumb clueless pushover as they are an evil manipulating bitch.

You Get What You Get!

These women, in my opinion, deserve whatever, and I mean this from the bottom of my nuttsack, WHATEVER the fuck happens to them in retaliation for their deceptive heartbreaking actions. These women are the wife-beaters of their gender, and I feel the same way about men who beat women.

Don't use and abuse a man, then be surprised if he tries to murder you and everyone you love. Humans are full of emotions and capable of anything. You cannot predict how one human will react when decided or hurt like that. Remember this, it's always the quiet one. Have you ever heard that before?

The quiet kid is the one that turns out to be the school shooter. The kids that were nice to him got that phone call the night before telling them don't come to school the next day.

It's the one that everyone always says "Well he doesn't seem like the type", that turns out to be exactly the type. Don't go throughout life thinking you're untouchable, cause it's gonna be a sad day when you finally get touched. God is forgiving, the universe is not, and they both very much so exist! Not every man you meet plays by the same rules, or is even mature enough to take on that level of heartbreak you dishing out. You will lose!

So don't gamble. Be honest from the jump, and don't let it get too far if you know in your heart this is not the man you want in your life or for your life. You'll end up wasting both of your time, and you also obtain the titles of a gold digger a manipulator, and a user. Kharma will come for you, and when she does, she gonna spank dat ass! Keep in mind what I said earlier in the book: dating is not about playing around. The human heart is not to be played with. If you want something to play with go buy a puppy!

Having a "Lil Attitude" Is Not Sexy

⚬⚭⚬

How do you feel when your little sister, your father, your bestie, or anyone for that matter catches an attitude with you? Likely you feel annoyed or upset! You may even feel let down or irritated, maybe some anxiety. Well, how do you think the so-called "love of your life" feels when you have an attitude 24/7 with them? You wake up angry or upset and the day hasn't even started yet. This is supposed to be your lover! Your Man! Your Person! Why is your way of showing them how much you love them by knocking years off their life with stress?

Grandma Vs. Pops

True story; My grandmother stressed my grandfather out until his last breath. He was a quiet and humble man who stayed out of the way. Very non-confrontational. My Grandma was very much the opposite; she was always in the mix, upsetting the family because of her strong opinion and inability to keep it to herself. A very interesting pair if you ask me. I know they loved each other, but they didn't always act like it. My grandma was always quick to let us know how much she couldn't stand my grandfather. Now that I think about it, maybe they hated each other, I guess I'll never know.

Over the years my grandfather became more and more of a homebody, primarily due to his bad knees and how much he still worked. My grandfather retired and then came out of retirement to continue supporting his family: the kids, the grand kids, even the great-grand kids. Plus my grandma had a cigarette and bingo addiction so he had to keep working so he could continue to fund her hobbies. Ion know if you're aware of this or not, but neither bingo nor cigarettes are cheap, especially when you do both daily!

For years while my grandfather was working, my grandma would take care of the house and kids. She already spent enough time in the house. Now she wanted to go outside, but Pops was like… naw. She resented him for that, among other things.

My grandma was a fireball! I remember seeing her yell at my grandfather while he was watching TV and my grandfather's calmness irritated my grandmother's soul! All he would ever respond to her with was " Okay Jackie". When get had enough he would just turn the TV off get up from his chair and walk away. No yelling, No cursing, just a very quiet and simple "Okay Jackie". This didn't sit well with my grandmother so she ran behind him as he was walking away and stabbed him in the back with a steak knife.

My grandfather being the man he is reacted in the most nonthreatening way a man could act in a situation like that. He turned around, pulled the knife out of his back, and said in the same quiet, calm tone "Calm Down Jackie." Then this man hands her back the steak knife and proceeds to continue walking away. He goes to the bathroom and cleans his wound, and my aunt stitches it for him. Then lays down for a nap. When he woke up, he walked into the kitchen and asked her what was for dinner, as if nothing had ever happened. My grandma hated that shit sooo much!!!

My grandma stressed my grandfather into an early grave, though not from the knife wound, his life was still eventually cut short due to the stress in it. It's not a day that goes by that my grandma doesn't wish she could have him back to do things differently. Grandma to this day thinks that my grandfather killed himself to try and get away from her.

For whatever reason, most women think that it's cute to stress out their men. They think it's gonna keep them around, keep them on their toes, or keep them interested. Whoever told you that Is most definitely in a toxic relationship. Truth is, men need to focus. They need to build their families, build for their families. Grow their savings and investments. Work on their careers and businesses! There's already so much on the plate of the modern-day man that the last thing he needs is for his woman to add anything up there that isn't fried chicken, collard greens, or mac & cheese.

Why stress your man out and push him closer to death when you can be his stress reliever when he comes home from getting beat up and bruised by the outside world? You can take care of him and help him extend his life and his fight. Think of yourself as a Cutman or I guess Cutwoman I should say. It's a position in boxing that if they are not there, the boxer will surely lose the fight. Have you ever seen a boxing match where the man fighting gets beat up pretty badly? His eye is swollen, he is bleeding from his eyebrow and his cheek, then he sits in his ring corner and there is a person there rubbing a metal plate on the fighter's face. This man with the metal plate is the Cutman. His job is to stop the bleeding, seal the cut, and open his eyes back up if they are swelling shut, helping him prepare to go back out there to finish the good fight that he is fighting. That Cutman is also a part of his team. That's what a woman should be to her man, his cutman!

If you're not helping him you're hurting him, and that makes you valueless to him. A waste of time and space in his life. Be his relief, be his peace! Why would you even want to add stress to him anyway? Don't you love him? Do you honestly think it's cute, walking around claiming to be "his biggest problem" or "his lil headache"? Did yo grandma teach you that? Is this what you and your friends talk about when you get together? It's time to grow up, and if you're reading this book I assume you're ready for the task.

Fear Vs. Anxiety

Maturing can be as straightforward or as hard as you make it. It may cause some anxiety, and might even be a little scary. Maybe you've already tried to no avail. It's all good momma, anxiety is a part of life but it doesn't have to control it! It also doesn't have to be a scary process. Keep this in mind, Though similar they are very different. Anxiety and Fear are siblings but they are not twins! Fear sees the danger, and Anxiety thinks about it.

Don't get caught up so much in your head thinking about times you may have failed trying to do exactly what you're reading about now. Maybe you've had a "lil attitude" all your life, since childhood. Well suck it up and be a big girl. Learn how to manage that temper and quick tongue, learn how to control their rude and unnecessary ass facial expressions. Learn where to direct these things! Life is filled with problems that need solving.

You got this,dont give up, wit yo disrespectful ass. Stop it with all the drama you seem to always cause. Don't be like my grandmother! Know that drama is not cute, it's just drama. No one ever said it was gonna be easy. Sometimes, the things in life that are worth having can be the most difficult to obtain and even more challenging to keep.

It takes consistent effort and fight on your part. Sometimes you can't even allow yourself to get comfortable. Comfortability provides room for a slip-up. Talk to your man, let him know your struggles, and see if you can come up with a solution together. That may be better than fighting the good fight of having a "lil attitude" on your own.

Plus it allows the opportunity for your man to express patience and give you more time and less worry to accomplish the goal you may have set with the subject. It will also please him knowing that you love and respect him enough to work on something he knows is not easy for you to just stop doing. That shows him your dedication to him the relationship and making this shit work! That's a turn-on and an excellent way to keep a good man around.

Self-Control

Push come to shove, just shut up. You start feeling that "lil attitude" coming shut that shit up. You got a feeling that your about to say some unnecessary slick shit, dead it before it starts. If you feel yourself getting upset in any way, shut up, walk away, or run away! You know for a fact that once you get upset, it's going to be a lot harder for you to think before you speak. This might sound harsh, but keep in mind this book was not created to cater to or spare your feelings; it's here to help the ones willing to listen and tell the truth to the women who are not afraid of it! Truth is, shutting up might just save your relationship. Keep in mind the story told in the chapter "Emotional Baggage Is Annoying" about the "Little Jimmy Bucket." Suppose you haven't learned how to control your mindset and your tongue yet. In that case, you'll just end up walking that stank attitude from relationship to relationship, slowly decreasing your value while blaming it on the other person. Trying to convince yourself you just haven't found the right one yet. Lying to yourself.

The truth is most people meet the person they are destined to be with forever before they even turn 25. So, if you are over 30 with this mindset, then it's time for you to do some soul-searching. If you are under 25, come on momma, I wanna see you win. You gotta be different from these other women and make that necessary change. You gotta have that something else, what is your something else?

Side Note: Today is Thursday, June 6th, 2024; on Tuesday, May 14th, 2024, My grandmother passed away. This is 1 Year and 4 Months after my Grandfather passed. For that year and a half of her life, she spent surrounded by her family and friends. Children, Grands, and Great-Grands. Though this tragedy deeply saddens the entire family, we also know that regardless of the abundance of love she had for us, all she truly just wanted was to be with her Husband, my grandfather, her prize. I love you, Grandma. I love you, Pops. I know I don't always get it right, but I hope I'm making you proud with my effort!

Today is 11/17/2025 And I Have No Idea What To Do With Myself. I Just Hope My Grandma Would Be Proud Of Me.

Yes! Flirting And Dancing Is Cheating!

Y'all really be tripping, tryna convince yourselves that you're not doing anything wrong when you go to those clubs and start rubbing your ass against another man's dick when you got a man at home, arousing him. No man wants his woman getting another man's dick hard especially not through physical contact. Yet a lot of women have convinced themselves there is nothing wrong with this hurtful and disgraceful act, and that it is far from cheating.

Imagine your man rubbing some random women's clit in the club? It's the same thing. Most folks are unaware because they chose not to educate themselves, but the clitoris and the penis are the same organs within males and females. This isn't me just talking, this is a scientific fact. So a woman grinding on a man's penis in the club is the same as a man rubbing a woman's clit in the club. Hopefully, this will give you something to think about.

The Golden Rule

Would you consider it cheating if your man was to do something like that? If your answer is no then this book will not help you find or keep the man you're looking for. You should probably be dating a drug dealer or any Jamaican man in a fishnet tank top. If your answer is yes, then I'm so proud of you for your learning, and you also have morals and are ready for some life changes.

Treat others how you want to be treated; no doubt many of us learned this saying or advice very early in life. It's what many people would refer to as the golden rule and even today, it still carries a lot of weight. Don't do anything to your man that you wouldn't want your man to do to you. This is how you establish trust between you two. Create your boundaries early, let him know what hurts you, what makes you cry, what is unforgivable to you, and then be woman enough not to do the same hurtful things to him. I mean, it just makes sense.

Think about it; you can't say things like, "I do not want you to go out to eat with your female coworker," then proceed to be the type of woman who thinks it's cute to have a work husband or allow a man at your job to be taking you out on your lunch break or even buying you lunch. Set boundaries; you are not so desperate for food or money that you need to say yes to these men offering food. Are you that hungry? Nah, your just that disrespectful. Don't try to justify the act by saying stupid things like, "If a man wants to buy me food, that's on him; who am I to say no."

Who Are You To Say "No"?

You are number 1, using that man and leading him on your own, which makes you a gold digger. You are also number 2, showing a lack of respect for your relationship and man. You're a woman trying to develop and maintain a robust and healthy relationship; that's who you are and why you should say no. What's wrong with you! No excuses! Treat others how you want to be treated. Men and women have specific roles that most of society is familiar with. Accepting free meals from that coworker is a form of courtship, And if you're in a relationship, then you're cheating. If you have no plans to be with the man buying you the food, then you're using him and deserve whatever happens to you on both ends.

Imagine discovering your man has been buying his female coworker lunch for the last two months. I'm talking Subway sandwiches and Chipotle burrito bowls. She has even been getting in the car with him on lunch break to go to the Chick-fil-A drive-through. Just think about it. How would that make you feel? I would assume it's not good. Well, it's the equivalent of you accepting meals from your coworker.

We all have roles; a man is a provider, and he provides for a multitude of reasons. Top court a woman, nurture a woman, impress a woman to protect his woman, make his woman happy, and make sure his family is safe and cared for. A woman's job is to accept or deny what that man is providing based on protection for him and their family and to help guide the man in the right direction. Also, I want to be there, support his decisions, and help strengthen him so he may continue to provide for her and the family. Do you want your man providing for another woman when he's supposed to be providing for you? So why would you think it's okay to allow another man to come into your life and play the role you've already chosen for your man to play? Do you just feel like being flirty today? Take your hoe ass to the city dump because that's where you belong.

Enough Games!

You playing games and do not take your relationship seriously. Be better than what you've already been in the past if your guilty of this act. If you've been fortunate enough to find a man who genuinely loves you and does right by you, then you owe it to him and yourself to properly accept the blessing you've been given. I promise you there are plenty of women that don't give a damn what your man looks like; they want him just because he is a good man. If you're mistreating him, then you lose him. Good men are rare, so if you get yourself one, act like you got some sense. Show him the same love, respect, and appreciation he shows you.

Don't hurt the man you claim you love just because you're used to doing whatever the hell your immature ass wants to do;

that's not law, and that's not right! You're wrong if you think it is. Treat that man how you want to be treated. Don't allow the world to convince you that a Queen can exist without a King. Though yes, your father can make you a princess, you will never become a Queen without first finding a real King; then you need to keep him. How do you keep him, you ask? Well, what's your something else? You see that, and you'll answer that question quickly.

Conclusion

Alright, ladies, we've made it to the end. If you made it this far, congrats! You either have thick skin, an open mind, or just enjoy being mad at the truth. Either way, you read it, and that means something.

So, what's the takeaway? Simple. Be real with yourself. Drop the delusions, take accountability, and understand that the world doesn't revolve around your feelings. Relationships are not built on entitlement, they are built on effort, compromise, and value. If you want a high-quality man, you need to be a high-quality woman. That means being self-aware, feminine,

126

supportive, and actually bringing something to the table other than demands. No you are not the fucking table!

Understand that men are not mind readers, nor are we emotional punching bags. If you keep making the same mistakes, attracting the same trash men, or struggling to find someone who wants to commit to you, then maybe, just maybe, the problem isn't every man in the world. Maybe it's you.

The Take Away

High body counts matter. Attitudes aren't cute. Single motherhood decreases your dating market value. Boss bitch energy isn't attractive to masculine men. And using men for what they can do for you will always backfire in the long run. These are just facts. Not opinions, not attacks, just reality. And if reality stings, that's a sign you need to change something.

The goal of this book wasn't to hurt you but to help you. To show you the truth women hate to hear but need to accept if they actually want the love and life they desire. If you apply even half of what's in this book, you'll be ahead of most women out here. You'll attract better men, maintain healthier relationships, and most importantly, respect yourself in a way that commands real love, not just temporary attention.

So now the ball's in your court. Will you take what you've learned and level up? Or will you stay stuck in the same cycle, blaming men, society, and everything else but yourself?

Will you be that difference men are looking for? That choice is yours. Just remember, delusion is expensive, but the truth is free. What's your something else? Choose wisely.

Disclaimer

The information provided in the book *"The Truth Women Hate to Hear"* is intended for general insight and educational purposes only.

About the Author

Conclusion

Glossary

Accountability – Taking responsibility for your actions and choices instead of blaming others.

Attention-Seeking – Behavior driven by the desire to be noticed or validated.

Baby Mama Drama – Conflict surrounding co-parenting, usually with an ex.

Beta Male – A weak, submissive man who lacks confidence and leadership.

Boss Bitch Energy – A mindset where a woman prioritizes her independence and dominance over cooperation in a relationship, often unattractive to masculine men.

Chameleon – A woman who changes her personality based on what a man wants.

Cheating – Engaging in romantic or sexual activity outside of a committed relationship.

Competition Anxiety – Fear of not being chosen due to other women being available.

Delusion – Convincing yourself something is reality when all evidence proves otherwise.

Double Standards – Societal expectations that differ for men and women.

Drama Queen – A woman who thrives on conflict and exaggerated emotional reactions.

Entitlement – Expecting things without putting in the necessary effort or value.

Emotional Baggage – Unresolved past trauma that negatively impacts relationships.

Feminine Energy – Embracing softness, supportiveness, and nurturing qualities.

Friend Zone – A situation where one person desires romance but the other only sees friendship.

Gold Digger – A woman primarily interested in a man for his financial resources.

Gaslighting – Manipulating someone into questioning their

reality.

High Body Count – Having had a large number of sexual partners, which can impact how men perceive a woman's relationship value.

Hypergamy – The practice of seeking a partner of higher status, often financial or social.

Independent Woman – A woman who can take care of herself but often struggles to balance relationships.

Insecurity – A lack of confidence leading to emotional instability.

Jealousy – A destructive emotion stemming from fear of losing someone's attention.

Keeper – A woman who possesses qualities that make her a great long-term partner.

Lady in the Streets – A woman who presents herself respectably in public but is passionate in private.

Loyalty – Faithfulness and commitment to one's partner.

Masculine Man – A man who embraces traditional masculinity, providing, protecting, and leading in relationships.

Marriage Material – A woman with qualities that make her suitable for long-term commitment.

Nice Guy – A man who is overly accommodating, often to his detriment.

Nurturing – A woman's ability to care for and support her partner emotionally.

OnlyFans – A platform often used for adult content, frequently discussed in modern dating.

Princess Complex – A mindset where a woman believes she is entitled to special treatment without contributing value.

Provider – A man who takes financial responsibility for his household.

Queen Energy – A woman who embodies confidence, grace, and value in her relationship.

Respect – Treating one's partner with honor and appreciation.

Red Flags – Warning signs of potential relationship problems.

Self-Respect – Holding yourself to a standard of behavior that ensures you receive proper treatment from others.

Single Mother – A woman raising children alone, which impacts dating prospects.

Submission – Willingness to trust and follow a strong, capable man's leadership in a relationship.

The Table – A metaphor for what a person brings to a relationship. Contrary to popular belief, just existing is not enough.
Toxic Femininity – When women use manipulation, victim hood, or entitlement to control relationships.

Ultimatum – Forcing a decision in a relationship under pressure.

Unrealistic Standards – Expecting perfection from a partner while not meeting the same criteria.

Validation – Seeking external approval to feel secure.

Wife Material – A woman with the qualities that make her an ideal long-term partner.

X-Factor – The unique quality that makes a woman stand out.

Zero Tolerance – Refusing to accept certain behaviors in relationships.

Bibliography

Quinn, Z. V. (2017). Escaping through the Past, Haunted by the Future: Confronting America through Child of God and the Underground Railroad. https://core.ac.uk/download/235422 648.pdf

If It Looks Like a Duck, Quacks Like a Duck and Walks Like a Duck, It's a Duck - Stoll Keenon Ogden PLLC. https://www.sk ofirm.com/publications/looks-like-duck-quacks-like-duck-w alks-like-duck-duck/

Unsolicited Relationship Advice - Josh Sherman. https://josht ronic.com/2019/03/15/unsolicited-relationship-advice/

Ideas for the book format - as well as the book table of contents - have also been taken from - "The Art Of Positive Thinking" - By Elizabeth R. Brown - ISBN/ 9798862579062

10 Reasons To Date The Girl Who's A Lady In The Streets But

A Freak In The Sheets. https://thoughtnova.com/10-reasons-to-date-the-girl-whos-a-lady-in-the-streets-but-a-freak-in-the-sheets

Recommended Reading

"The Art of Positive Thinking" by Elizabeth R. Brown

"Becoming Your Own Banker" by R. Nelson Nash

"A Deeper Love Inside" by Sister Souljah

"The Art of Traveling Cheap" Written by LaTre'

"Onlybandz: How To Become A Pornstar" Written by LaTre'

"The Power Of Kindness" Written By LaTre'

About the Author

LaTrè is a critical thinker, strategist, and entrepreneur who has spent years dissecting the complexities of modern relationships, attraction, and human nature. With an analytical mind and a no-nonsense approach, he breaks down the uncomfortable truths most people are too afraid to confront. His insights are not based on theory but on real-world experience, research, and an unfiltered understanding of human behavior.

With a background that spans entertainment, fitness coaching, and personal development, LaTrè brings a unique perspective that blends psychology, social dynamics, and raw honesty. The Truth Women Hate to Hear isn't just another relationship book, it's a wake-up call. Through sharp analysis and undeniable facts, LaTrè exposes the patterns shaping today's dating world and forces readers to see reality for what it truly is.

You can connect with me on:

🌐 https://midnitedakota.com